EUCHARISTIC WORSHIP

in Ecumenical Contexts

EUCHARISTIC WORSHIP

in Ecumenical Contexts

THE LIMA LITURGY - AND BEYOND

Edited by
Thomas F. Best and Dagmar Heller

WCC Publications, Geneva

Cover design: Raphael Michaluk/AGL
Cover illustration: Batik, "The Last Supper" by Solomon Raj. © *One World –
Christian Art*. Used by permission.

Music typeset by Terry MacArthur and Ulisses Mantovani

ISBN 2-8254-1232-5

© 1998 WCC Publications, World Council of Churches,
150 route de Ferney, 1211 Geneva 2, Switzerland

Printed in Switzerland

Table of Contents

I

Introduction

Editors' Introduction

This book records the experience of a community of liturgists, theologians, church musicians, pastors and others gathered in the setting of the Ecumenical Institute, Bossey, near Geneva, Switzerland, 12-21 May 1995, to reflect on – and look beyond – one of the phenomena of the modern ecumenical movement: the eucharistic service known as the Lima liturgy.

The goals of the meeting were, first, to review and reflect upon the experience gained by the churches in using the Lima liturgy since its introduction in 1982, to consider this experience from both the theological and the liturgical points of view, and in light of this to suggest principles for eucharistic celebrations in ecumenical settings; and second, to produce such new material for use in the churches and especially, where possible according to church discipline, in ecumenical contexts.

The members of this gathered community – with different experience and service in the church, the world and the ecumenical movement, of varying ages and Christian confessions, lay and ordained – all shared an interest in worship generally and in eucharistic worship in particular. Participants from all regions of the globe contributed to our work: apart from Europe and North America, the largest number came from Latin America and their challenging voice was an important stimulus to the work of the consultation. They came primarily from Protestant and Anglican confessions, because, broadly speaking, it is those whose members are able officially to share the eucharist across confessional boundaries, and thus to participate together in the Lima liturgy. But there was Roman Catholic and Orthodox presence also, reminding the consultation of the limits which still exist upon our participation at the table of the Lord.

The results of this meeting are published on behalf of the consultation itself; they do not represent the official position of the WCC or of any of its programmes. Nevertheless, the meeting drew extensively upon participants and results from recent ecumenical work on worship; it takes forward, we believe, the ecumenical discussion on eucharistic worship; and we publish the following texts in the hope – indeed, with the conviction – that they will be useful to the churches and to the ecumenical movement.

The Lima liturgy: an ecumenical milestone

Just what is the Lima liturgy, and why does it seem to hold such promise for the churches' eucharistic worship and their search for visible unity? It was produced for use as the closing worship at the World Council of Churches' Faith and

Order plenary commission meeting in Lima, Peru, in 1982,[1] the meeting from which Faith and Order sent *Baptism, Eucharist and Ministry*[1] to the churches for study and response at the "highest appropriate level".[2] *BEM*, as it quickly became known, recorded theological convergence among a wide range of churches on many aspects of baptism, eucharist and ministry, and clarified issues needing further discussion.

The Lima liturgy was intended as a "liturgical expression of convergence achieved in *Baptism, Eucharist and Ministry*".[3] But this "liturgical expression" did more than *embody* many of the churches' common convictions about the meaning and practice of the eucharist or Lord's supper. It also enabled Christians to *experience*, in a setting of shared prayer and praise, these fruits of a growing communion among the churches. "Ecumenical progress" became not just something to be written about; it could be prayed and sung together with others, and this at the central moment of Christian worship, while gathered together, at Christ's invitation, around the table of the Lord. As one church leader said: "What people in my church know about *BEM* they learned not from *BEM* itself, but from sharing together in the Lima liturgy."

Two important clarifications – and qualifications – must be made. First, the Lima liturgy is an *unofficial* text – it was, by intention, never formally voted on or adopted by Faith and Order, nor was it sent officially to the churches as was *BEM* itself. There are many and complex reasons for this. Faith and Order has focussed on the underlying theological (rather than liturgical) reasons for the divisions among the churches. Many of the most sensitive theological and ecclesiological issues come to focus in the eucharistic event, and Faith and Order did not want to claim official status for a particular eucharistic text, whatever its qualities. Nor did Faith and Order want to give the impression that it had any authority to "authorize" a particular eucharistic text, for that authority belongs to the churches alone.

Yet the Lima liturgy has evoked an immediate and growing response, one far beyond any expectations of those who had crafted it. It has corresponded to, and resonated with, such a widespread and deep-seated hunger among Christians in the separated churches that it has been widely used for eucharistic worship at countless ecumenical events, from parish level to WCC assemblies. Offering a dignified and rich eucharistic service, it draws on a wide range of liturgical resources in a way that is both respectful of the tradition and open to the future. It has led many Christians to a deeper understanding of the Lord's supper as a liturgical event rooted in the life of the church and its tradition. It has stimulated discussion among liturgists about the form and content of the eucharistic event. And not least – though this was far from the original intent – it has posed a challenge to the churches: unofficial it may be, but the extent and depth of the response it has evoked calls the churches to urgent further work on the issues which keep so many of us divided at the Lord's table.

For, second, we *are* still divided at the Lord's table. The Lima liturgy did not, and could not, perform theological and ecclesiological miracles. Specifically the Lima liturgy does not enable "intercommunion", that is, the sharing of the eucharist by those whose churches are not in full communion and differ fundamentally in their understanding of the nature, meaning and administration of the eucharist. Where fundamental differences remain in the understanding of the eucharist and of who can properly preside at it, these must be solved by the churches concerned before they can join together at the Lord's table. What the Lima Liturgy *does* do is to embody, in broad terms, the common understanding of the eucharist held by a wide range of churches, Protestant and Anglican, who because they do agree fundamentally about the eucharist are able to join together at the Lord's table. It reflects – and has come to symbolize – the theological convergence among these churches and their resulting ability to share together at the Lord's table. And in this it is a powerful symbol of hope for all Christians.

Beyond the Lima liturgy

After more than a decade since the introduction of the Lima liturgy it seemed time to take stock of the experience gained in its widespread use, and the intensive discussion which it had generated among liturgists and worship leaders. Church leaders, theologians and liturgists alike were asking questions such as: What could be learned from the widespread use of the Lima liturgy? What *were* the theological, liturgical and human needs which it was meeting? Had the experience with the Lima liturgy created a new theological or liturgical situation, within some churches at least?

And again: What was the experience of the Lima liturgy as *liturgy*? What was its contribution? What about comments that it was too didactic, wordy, elaborate? Could the proposals originally included with the Lima liturgy for simplifying and adapting it be more widely circulated and used? Could the experience with the Lima liturgy yield principles for holding eucharistic worship in ecumenical contexts, principles which could guide those charged with developing such worship? Could the Lima liturgy be improved or, better, could we "harvest" this widespread experience to develop new eucharistic services reflecting the ecumenical advances, both theological and liturgical, which have been made even since the Lima liturgy was written?

Such were the questions facing the community gathered at Bossey, questions touching upon fundamental aspects of the faith and life of the church.

The meeting and its results: a "reader's guide" to this book

As befitted the diverse gifts of its participants, the meeting was a combination of *seminar* (receiving and producing texts on eucharistic theology and practice for study and discussion) and *workshop* (experiencing and producing materials intended for practical use in the eucharistic worship of the churches). This book endeavours to reflect this twofold structure of the meeting, and the different types of material received and produced. It begins with a personal account by one participant, Rodney Matthews, which well serves to introduce the vision and dynamic of our time together.

Material for reflection on eucharistic worship

Section II then focusses on the churches' experience with the Lima liturgy and suggests possible further steps in eucharistic worship in ecumenical contexts. The section begins with the two main papers presented to the meeting, the first an account of the "Origin, Intention and Structure" of the Lima liturgy by Max Thurian. Fr Max was, of course, one of the principal architects of the Lima liturgy as well as of *BEM* itself. By outlining its genesis, its intention and the liturgical sources for its various parts, he took the consultation into the "heart" of the Lima liturgy as originally understood by those who shaped it. This was one of the last public presentations made by Fr Max before his death in 1996, and his insights into the origins and intention of the Lima liturgy, his gracious responses in an extended question-and-answer session afterwards, and his very presence lent a special quality to our time together.

The incisive paper by Gordon Lathrop, "Moving Forward Ecumenically", then invites the churches to claim, as their common heritage, the eucharistic experience of the early church; to focus together on the classic *ordo* (shape or pattern) of the eucharistic service; and to share with one another the ancient and contemporary material, particularly the eucharistic prayers, which shape their present eucharistic practice. Characteristically of Gordon Lathrop, this gracious "invitation" bears more than a hint of challenge to the churches!

For its subsequent work the consultation divided into several groups, and the text "Celebrations of the Eucharist in Ecumenical Contexts: A Proposal" records the work of one of these. This group sought to continue recent ecumenical work on worship, particularly the reflections of the Faith and Order Ditchingham consultation[4] on the role of worship in the search for Christian unity. Starting from Christian tradition and the convergence reached in *BEM*, it focussed on issues of the *ordo* (shape or pattern) of the eucharistic service, and of inculturation. The group report offers not a new eucharistic text but suggestions as to the liturgical *spirit* in which the service is conducted, thus complementing the theological focus of *BEM* through the insights of those specially sensitive to the *liturgical* dimensions of the eucharistic service.[5] Though addressed primarily to an ecumenical audience, the text could help churches reflect upon their own eucharistic practice. The text is printed here in the original English and, to encourage wider discussion, also in German and Spanish; French and Swedish versions are available upon request from Faith and Order. The section concludes with the text of the Lima liturgy, reprinted here to facilitate discussion and study.

Material for use in eucharistic worship

Section III is comprised of worship materials produced for, at or in connection with the consultation. In all, the consultation shared in six eucharistic services, of which we are able here to print four. These services nourished our common life and reminded us of our link with the wider church; they also served as a source for the reflection upon the eucharist, and provided an opportunity for our reflections and suggestions to be put into immediate liturgical practice.

After each service (except of course that which concluded our meeting) the consultation undertook the sensitive and difficult task of reflecting on the worship which it had just experienced. This was not an exercise in dissection; reverence was called for, for we were dealing with honest efforts to enter the presence of God, to share in the mysteries of our faith. It was intended to instruct and deepen the life and work of the community, and to help participants prepare more effective services in the future. The consultation sought to understand how each service had functioned as *liturgy*, and how it might have been done otherwise, perhaps more effectively. Participants asked one another, respectfully yet sometimes forcefully, questions such as: Was the service well constructed and led? Did it lead the worshippers into the presence of God? Was the word faithfully and powerfully proclaimed? Was there a clear sense of Christ's presence at his table? How might the prayers have been shaped, the service led, to lead worshippers in the Spirit more immediately to God and to Christ? Was the service, as it sought to express the faith in the forms of a particular culture, yet faithful to the tradition of the church through the ages? What are the possibilities, and limits, for expressing the eucharistic service in local cultural forms? How may specific concerns for the world's well-being, in particular issues of justice, peace and the care for creation, be brought into the eucharistic service in a way that clarifies rather than obscures or overshadows the presence of Christ, and the life which Christ offers to the world?

The section begins with two eucharistic services which had been prepared for the meeting by participants from particular regions of the world. They had been asked to develop services based upon the Lima liturgy, but expressed in a form appropriate to their own confessional and cultural context. We have retained the original form of the eucharistic service from Latin America, a substantial portion of which was prepared in Spanish. In a later stage of its worship and work the consultation shared in eucharistic services developed by groups working at the meeting, in light of our common reflection and liturgical experience. The first of these printed here emphasizes the theme of spiritual growth, both personal and communal.

These eucharistic services conclude with an account of the consultation's closing worship. This service is not represented by a text because, remarkably, there *was* no text; the entire service was conducted without paper. For many it was the climactic experience of our life together. Drawing on familiar ancient and recent eucharistic texts, including contemporary materials familiar to many in the congregation, allowing ample space for participation, and introduced and led clearly by the presiding and assisting ministers, this hour-long service freed the worshippers to focus on prayer and praise of God, the receiving of the bread and wine, prayer for one another and for the world, and the mission and service to the world to follow. In the absence of a text for the service, Rodney Matthews has provided an account which conveys much of the progress and impact of this closing service.

The section continues with a "Mass for Our Time" by two of the participants in the consultation, Kurt Rose and Wolfgang Teichmann (to encourage wider use of the material we are pleased to print it in the original German as well as in an English translation), prayers from one of the eucharists prepared during the consultation, and eucharistic and non-eucharistic worship materials by participant Per Harling.

Next follows a statement of "Affirmations about Ecumenical Worship" by Robert Gribben. This text, written at and in light of the consultation, looks at the broader worship life of the churches, seeking to summarize and focus principles from ecumenical practice and reflection which could guide the churches' worship life.

Section IV is an appendix offering a rich collection of "Material for Reflection on the Structure and Content of the Eucharistic Service". This material illustrates the broad liturgical principles underlying the text "Celebrations of the Eucharist in Ecumenical Contexts: A Proposal"; it should also be read in connection with the paper by Gordon Lathrop and the Lima liturgy. In terms of programmatic proposals made by Gordon Lathrop, the material may aid the churches' reflection on the *shape* or *structure* of the eucharistic service, and encourage them to share the agreed ancient and contemporary eucharistic texts, particularly texts of the eucharistic prayer, which they are currently using.

Finally, the cover of this book reflects an important moment in the consultation, a stimulating evening in which the Indian Christian artist Solomon Raj displayed and explained his work in the media of batik. In bold, colourful images this art seeks to convey the meaning of Christian faith through the idioms of Indian culture. This raised powerful issues of inculturation, and of art as a means for expressing religious experience and truth. In discussion, the artist underscored also the importance of the *space* in which the eucharist is celebrated, an issue which deserves far more attention than it usually receives. We are grateful to Solomon Raj, and to *One World – Christian Art*, for permission to use for our cover design the artist's interpretation of the last supper.

The dynamic of the meeting: a comment

Every meeting has its own dynamic and its inevitable share of difficulties. This consultation undertook a special challenge in bringing together participants from widely differing perspectives, and with strongly held convictions, to work in the complex and sensitive field of eucharistic worship. To some extent the twin aspects of the meeting – its character as *seminar* on the one hand, and *workshop* on the other – stood in tension. The consultation worked hard to hold liturgical reflection and practice together. Differing levels of ecumenical awareness and sensitivity, too, had to be integrated within the community. All these could serve as constructive and creative tensions, because the community was held together by two common convictions: that the eucharist stands at the heart of the church's life, and that the issues of eucharistic worship are among the most important facing the ecumenical movement.

Thanks and conclusion

We would like to express heartfelt thanks to those who planned the consultation and carried it through with us: to our staff colleagues Terry MacArthur and Beate Stierle, and to Janet Crawford from New Zealand. We thank all those who participated in the consultation and contributed to its programme and results, as well as the staff of the Ecumenical Institute, Bossey. Special thanks go to Carolyn McComish for her work in preparing the text for publication.

We are pleased to record here our thanks to Klaus Wilkens, ecumenical officer of the Evangelical Church in Germany, whose continuing insistence on the importance of the Lima liturgy was one of the principal inspirations for the consultation. And we express deep gratitude to the WCC member churches which provided generous financial support for the meeting: the Evangelical Church in Germany, the Presbyterian Church (USA), the Episcopal Church [USA], the United Methodist Church [USA] and the Christian Church (Disciples of Christ) [USA].

We hope that this account of the Lima liturgy seminar and workshop will stimulate wide reflection within and among the churches on their eucharistic worship, how it can more evidently be a sign of the presence of God, and how it can reflect and foster that unity which is ours as members together of the one body of Christ.

THOMAS F. BEST   DAGMAR HELLER

NOTES

[1] *Baptism, Eucharist and Ministry*, Faith and Order paper no. 111, Geneva, WCC, 1982. Translated into more than 35 languages and the subject of more than 180 official church responses, *Baptism, Eucharist and Ministry* is the most widely discussed ecumenical text of recent years.

[2] *Ibid.*, "Preface", p.x.

[3] See "The Eucharistic Liturgy: Liturgical Expression of Convergence in Faith Achieved in Baptism, Eucharist and Ministry", Geneva, WCC, 1983; also available as "The Eucharistic Liturgy of Lima", in *Ecumenical Perspectives on Baptism, Eucharist and Ministry*, Max Thurian, ed., Faith and Order paper no. 116, Geneva, WCC, 1983, appendix II, pp.224-46. Strikingly, the original publication of the Lima liturgy included suggestions for "possible simplifications" in order to focus the text and to enable its use in a variety of situations.

[4] *So We Believe, So We Pray: Towards Koinonia in Worship*, Thomas F. Best and Dagmar Heller, eds, Faith and Order paper no. 171, Geneva, WCC, 1995. See also Thomas F. Best and Janet Crawford, "Praise the Lord with the Lyre... and the Gamelan?", in *The Ecumenical Review*, vol. 46, no. 1, Jan. 1994, pp.78-96; and *Worshipping Ecumenically: Orders of Service from Global Meetings with Suggestions for Local Use*, Per Harling, ed., Geneva, WCC, 1995.

[5] See especially *Baptism, Eucharist and Ministry, op. cit.*, Eucharist, para. 27. It is symptomatic that the list of aspects of the eucharistic service indicates neither their relative significance, nor which aspects are essential to the service and which optional, nor their place within the structure of the service as a whole.

A Participant's Introduction
Ecumenical Liturgy in Principle and Practice

RODNEY MATTHEWS

Kastanienblüten	Chestnut blossoms
Kalter Tag im Mai	Cold a day in May
in der Kapelle	and in the chapel
Singen, Schweigen, Beten	singing, silence, praying

Kurt Rose, workshop participant

Between Easter and Ascensiontide 1995 a community of Christ's people were drawn from the four corners of the earth to gather at the Ecumenical Institute, Bossey, Switzerland. For ten days this group of 35 sat together under God's word read and proclaimed, issuing in profound reflection and response. We gave thanks to God for his unspeakable goodness as together at table we ate and drank the holy gifts of creation and the work of human hands. We were then sent back to the disparate communities from which we had come, charged with living and witnessing to the experience of our renewal in Christ, in whom alone we found unity shining through our diversity.

This fourfold action – gathering, word, table, being sent – held us in the firm framework for the deliberate task to which we had been called. It is the same pattern which every Sunday unites Christians the world over in local assemblies and in continuity through the ages.

For us, as for every Christian meeting, the purpose was particular, yet in the context of the universal. We had come, some by appointment, others by open invitation, to try to help the churches take a further step together in the ecumenical pilgrimage by reviewing the Lima liturgy. This was first produced on behalf of the World Council of Churches in 1982 to express, in a liturgical setting, the theological convergence reached on baptism, eucharist and ministry.

This Lima liturgy has subsequently been used far beyond the original version, both in world assemblies – at Vancouver 1983 and Canberra 1991 – and as a model for smaller ecumenical gatherings. Following the fifth world conference on Faith and Order at Santiago de Compostela, Spain, in 1993, a further consultation on "Towards Koinonia in Worship: The Role of Worship within the Search for Unity" held at Ditchingham, England, in 1994[1] recommended that this liturgy be reviewed, partly with future world assemblies in mind but more particularly because of significant developments in Christian relationships over the past 15 years.

Not the least of these factors have been a growing awareness of the diversity of our cultures and contexts and the rich variety of resources which are God's gifts to and in his people.

Both these elements found expression in the gathering at Bossey, for here, in addition to some who had shared in the Ditchingham experience, were drawn together musicians, poets and artists, as well as theologians, ecclesiologists and liturgists. In this coming together we were made aware of the gifts of rich and poor; young and old; black and white; male and female; pastors and those whose ministry is exercised in the secular world; Orthodox, Catholic and Reformed. Whilst in no sense could this gathering be regarded as an even-handed representation of every possible grouping, we were a variety of Christians responding to God's call to draw together work and worship in genuine liturgy. In this we were typical of any assembly at any time.

It soon became evident that we did not come empty-handed, but carried burdens as well as gifts. We found it difficult to separate "the good from the bad" – the evidence of God's blessing in our lives, yet also the sins of the world to which we cling. At least in this way our gathering was representative for, like the two on the Emmaus road, we began by admitting that, in spite of all the promises received, life in the world in which we lived fell short of that for which we hoped and prayed.

Now, like those disciples, we learnt anew something of the living word which creates, redeems and transforms. It is always a painful process. Disunity cannot be resolved through accusation and argument. In the clamour for many voices to be heard we sometimes risked drowning the one clear holy voice which alone could unite. We hurt each other. In the struggle over power we failed to recognize the nature of the authority of the servant in our midst. Yet living the paradox of the gospel, we also discovered that when we were ready to empty ourselves we were able to receive what was being offered. When we drew near to Christ we drew near to each other and in the affirmation of this unity we were empowered to pray together for others in Christ's name.

So to the table where, living together as we were, served by the unassuming staff and volunteer "blue angels" of the Château at Bossey, we met constantly to break bread, thankful for all God provides. As we looked across the lake to snow-capped mountains we were deeply conscious of the beauty of creation and we lamented transient ugliness as well, for that belongs also to our view. We were filled with hope through signs of the coming of the kingdom as we tasted and saw that the Lord is good. This hope was reflected in joy.

It was in such a living, eucharistic context that we tried to recognize and express the unity which holds together our diversity. Those who had been at Ditchingham had found that a vivid rainbow symbolized the mystery of divine wholeness shining through variety. One day that rainbow shone over Lake Geneva. For all its multi-colour and diffusion it cannot be fractured. It is impossible for the colours to be isolated from each other. As we worked together we were drawn into a holistic pattern: liturgical principle born out in practice; textual expression in the context of real experience; flesh and soul together. The broken world from which we had come was seen to be restored in the living Christ in our midst.

The integrity of this experience was expressed in our final eucharist, celebrated without any denominational books or papers that so often stifle or inhibit worship, especially in a multicultural, multilingual, ecumenical assembly. Our bodies were free to the promptings of our spirits. Yet both the shape and content of the service would have satisfied liturgical purist and theological dogmatician alike. More than at any other time we were here united as Christ's "new creation". We lived out in practice what we have tried to set down here in print – in fact, all that follows in this account.

At last, at the point of being sent to witness to what had happened to us, with the spontaneity of those recognizing the Christ in the home at Emmaus, we went on our way, undertaking far-flung journeys, dispersing on the four winds to those waiting in hope and prayer for a better day to dawn. The journey is not over but is full of promise. We might have said,

> We shall not cease from exploration,
> And the end of all our exploring
> Will be to arrive where we started
> And know the place for the first time.[2]

NOTES

[1] Thomas F. Best and Dagmar Heller, eds, *So We Believe, So We Pray*, Geneva, WCC, Faith and Order paper no. 171, 1995.
[2] T.S. Eliot, "Little Gidding" from "Four Quartets", *The Complete Poems and Plays 1909-1950*, New York, Harcourt, Brace & Co., 1958, p. 145.

II

Reflections on the Lima Liturgy
and Proposals
for Moving Ahead

The Lima Liturgy
Origin, Intention and Structure

MAX THURIAN

When I was asked in October 1981 to prepare the eucharistic liturgy for the meeting of the World Council of Churches' Faith and Order plenary commission, which was to be held in Lima, Peru, in January 1982, I had considerable reservations. The idea was that the liturgy should illustrate the theological results achieved in the document "Baptism, Eucharist and Ministry", the final draft of which was about to be approved. That aspect of the undertaking interested me greatly, for since 1967 I had been actively involved in working out the convergence text which later came to be called *BEM (Baptism, Eucharist and Ministry).*[1] But on the other hand I was hesitant about embarking on the adventure of liturgical composition, which was not to my taste: to my mind, a liturgy comes to us from the experience of tradition rather than being composed to reflect a particular set of theological ideas. In the end, I decided to accept the assignment and to adopt a method that would honour the intention of illustrating the *BEM* document while also showing all due respect for the liturgical tradition of the church, the people of God's experience of prayer throughout the ages. I searched traditional liturgical documents for elements that would correspond to the main points of *BEM*.

This was particularly important as far as the eucharistic prayer or *anaphora* was concerned. For the prayers, collects and thanksgiving after communion, the kyrie litany, the prayer of intercession and the preface I could allow myself greater freedom to compose according to the theme. The balance between respect for tradition and creative freedom determines whether or not a liturgy is really "received" by the people of God, in other words, whether it really corresponds to the experience of a Christian community prayer. Time will tell whether this Lima liturgy can be "received" in the church as a genuine common prayer. It was celebrated at Lima on 15 January 1982, then at the WCC central committee on 28 July 1982, presided over by the WCC general secretary, Philip Potter, and again at the sixth assembly of the World Council in Vancouver on 31 July 1983, with the archbishop of Canterbury, Dr Runcie, as presiding minister, to mention only the major occasions. In Vancouver the Lima liturgy was well received.

The second idea behind this liturgy was to allow as many Christians as possible to participate and to enable ministers from as many church traditions as possible to take an active part in the celebration. This is why the liturgy is clearly divided into two main parts: the liturgy of the word and the liturgy of the

---

• Translated from the French by the WCC Language Service.

eucharist. All the churches represented in the World Council of Churches, and the Roman Catholic Church, can participate in the liturgy of the word and the liturgy of entrance without any problem. The gospel was thus proclaimed in various languages by different Orthodox metropolitans at the central committee meeting in Geneva and, at Vancouver, by the Roman Catholic bishop of Würzburg, amongst others. This sharing in the liturgy of entrance and the liturgy of the word underlines our deep communion in the one baptism and in the one holy scripture, even if we cannot yet all concelebrate and share at the same eucharistic table. This should not be seen simply as a charitable concession but as a genuine act of communion, as we recall our one baptism and listen to the same word of God contained in the holy scripture of the Old and New Testaments.

While some cannot participate fully in the eucharistic liturgy for reasons of faith, concerning in particular the apostolic ministry, one could perhaps reinstate here the practice of spiritual, non-sacramental communion or the distribution of consecrated bread. As for those who feel free to take communion together or even to concelebrate, they should remember that this cannot be done lightly but must flow from a common faith which, to be authentic, must be in obedience to the intention of Christ and in conformity with the tradition of the apostles.

In Vancouver, the presiding minister, the archbishop of Canterbury, was assisted by six ministers (including two ordained women) representing different church traditions: Lutheran (from Denmark), Reformed (from Indonesia), Methodist (from Benin), Baptist (from Hungary), Moravian (from Jamaica), and the United Church of Canada. It should be noted, however, that this was not a "concelebration" in the technical sense of the term (contrary to certain reports in the press). For one thing, the different officiants belonged to churches some of which do not have concelebration and, for another, we did not want to embarrass the archbishop of Canterbury. The six people officiating at the eucharist were "assisting ministers", as we called them. The archbishop of Canterbury pronounced the whole of the eucharistic prayer, with the assisting ministers joining him for the anamnesis and the second epiclesis. The assisting ministers also shared the offertory and communion prayers among themselves. But something which often happens in the Roman Catholic liturgy at the conclusion of the eucharistic prayer (the *per ipsum*) also happened in Vancouver. When the archbishop and the assisting ministers began to pray together, many people in the congregation spontaneously joined in. This liturgical faux-pas has to be interpreted in a positive sense, as reflecting the common desire to participate in the liturgy in which everyone had been deeply involved.

The liturgy of entrance

This liturgy of preparation emphasizes the communion of all Christians in the royal and prophetic priesthood received at their common baptism with water and with the Spirit. It is an illustration of Peter's words:

> But you are a chosen race, a royal priesthood, a holy nation, God's own people, in order that you may proclaim the mighty acts of him who called you out of darkness into his marvellous light. Once you were not a people, but now you are God's people; once you had not received mercy, but now you have received mercy (1 Pet. 2:9-10).

This marks the gathering of God's people, so often recalled in the Psalms: "... I went with the throng, and led them in procession to the house of God, with glad shouts and songs of thanksgiving, a multitude keeping festival" (Ps. 42:4). A procession of all the community, or at least of all those leading the service, best symbolizes this gathering of the church, foreshadowing the eschatological gathering of God's people in the kingdom. This entrance is accompanied by a psalm sung by the "people proclaiming the Lord's praise". The presiding minister then greets the assembled people in the words of the liturgy of the primitive church as given to us by St Paul: "The grace of the Lord Jesus Christ, the love of God, and the communion of the Holy Spirit be with you all" (2 Cor. 13:13), calling them "from darkness into God's wonderful light", as they receive his mercy in the confession of sins and absolution. These two texts are taken from the North American Lutheran liturgy. Noteworthy in the words of absolution is the reference to the ordained ministry of the church which, on Christ's authority, can declare the entire forgiveness of sins (cf. *BEM*, Ministry, 15). The confession of sins is spoken in unison by the whole congregation, and the absolution is given by the presiding minister.

This is followed by the *kyrie* and the *gloria*, two quite traditional elements in Western liturgies. These illustrate the two fundamental aspects of Christian prayer – supplication and praise. The kyrie is in the form of a short litany. In Lima and in Vancouver, the three intentions of this litany were:
- the one baptism of Christians, that it might lead them to maintain the unity of the Spirit (Eph. 4:3-5);
- the communion of the eucharist, from which we may draw the strength to attain to visible communion in the body of Christ (1 Cor. 10:16-17);
- the mutual recognition of ministries in our reconciliation to God through Christ (2 Cor. 5:18-20).

The petitions of this litany could vary according to circumstances. It was also foreseen that the short penitential litany in the present Roman Catholic liturgy, or the opening litany of the liturgy of St John Chrysostomos, could replace this *kyrie* litany.

The *gloria in excelsis* represents praise and contemplation following upon supplication. It can be sung in unison or alternately. In the latter case, as for the petitions in the kyrie litany, it is preferable that another officiant, either a minister or a lay person, should dialogue with the congregation.

The liturgy of the word

This part of the celebration of the eucharist goes from the collect to the prayer of intercession.

The *collect* is a kind of epiclesis on the scripture readings and the sermon, asking that these may become genuinely God's word for us. It varies according to the circumstances and the theme of the readings. In Lima it once again evoked the three subjects of *BEM*: the anointing of Christ by the Spirit at his baptism in the Jordan, consecrating him as prophet, priest and king; the renewal of the Spirit which makes us ardently desire the communion of the body and blood of Christ (Luke 22:15); and the ministry of the church which is first of all for the poor of God's people.

The *first reading* is taken from the Old Testament or from the Acts of the Apostles or from the Revelation. In Lima, the text chosen was Ezekiel 47:1-9 on the water from below the threshold of the temple, recalling the purifying, cleansing, life-giving immersion of baptism. The hymn of meditation which follows is generally part of a psalm, sung responsively.

The *second reading* is taken from an epistle. In Lima this was the first letter of Peter (5:1-11), on the theme of ministry. The *alleluia* then resounds as an acclamation hailing the gospel, after which the gospel is proclaimed by a deacon or by the third reader. In Lima, the gospel reading was the Emmaus narrative (Luke 24:25-32) and the eucharistic meal was preceded by the interpretation of the scriptures.

The homily expounds the message of God's word for today; it is the voice of the church, echoing that of the prophets, of the apostles and of Christ. A time of silence allows everyone to meditate in their hearts on the word received.

After this the *creed* is said or sung, summarizing the history of salvation. This can be the Nicene Creed or the Apostles' Creed. Out of an ecumenical spirit of faithfulness to the original text we give here, as in Lima, at the central committee in Geneva and in Vancouver, the text of the council of Constantinople (in 381). The commemoration of this in 1981 reinstated this early text which reconciles East and West in the fundamentals of the faith.

We would like to see this version of the Nicene-Constantinopolitan Creed included in liturgical books alongside the Western version and the Apostles' Creed, as a sign of openness towards the East on the part of the West, and of regret for an historical "error". This would not imply a uniformization of pneumatological concepts (a forced uniformity in the understanding of the Holy Spirit) in the different theologies. A proposal to this effect was presented at the International Congress on Pneumatology in Rome in 1981.

Intercession draws the believing community together, nourished by the word of God, uniting it in prayer for all the needs of the church and of the world. The structure and style adopted here are those of the litany of Pope Gelasius (+ 496), representing the kyrie in use in Rome at the end of the 5th century.[2] The six intentions here are: the invocation of the Holy Spirit for the church; the leaders of the nations, justice and peace; those who suffer oppression and violence; then, based on the themes of *BEM*: the unity of the church in baptism; the communion of the churches around the one table; mutual recognition by the churches of each other's ministries.

The liturgy of the eucharist

The liturgy of the eucharist begins with the presentation of the bread and the wine, accompanied by two blessings from the Jewish liturgy (taken up in the revised Roman Catholic liturgy) and by a prayer inspired by the Didachè. The very ancient Aramaic eucharistic acclamation "Maranatha" ("Come, Lord!" or "The Lord comes!", 1 Cor. 16:22) concludes this preparation.

The eucharistic prayer begins with a preface based likewise on the theme of *BEM*. First, the thanksgiving for creation focusses on the word which gives life, especially to human beings who reflect God's glory. When the time is accomplished, Christ is given as the Way, the Truth and the Life. In the history of Jesus, the preface evokes the consecration of God's Servant through baptism, the last supper of the eucharist, the memorial of the death, resurrection and presence of the Saviour given to us as food. Lastly, the preface mentions the gift of the royal priesthood to all Christians, among whom God chooses the ministers who will feed the church with the word and by the sacraments, that it may live.

The invocation of the Holy Spirit upon "our eucharist" is an *epiclesis* on the bread and the wine, and on the whole worshipping community, ministers and faithful. The epiclesis is derived from Jesus' words at the institution of the Lord's supper, according to the Alexandrine tradition and the Roman tradition.[3]

Depending on the traditions, the epiclesis is placed either before Christ's words of institution ("This is my body... This cup is my blood..."), thus demonstrating the action of the Holy Spirit making the words of the Son present and effective to the glory of the Father; or after the *anamnesis* of the mysteries of salvation, thus demonstrating the gift of the Spirit completing the work of the Father and the Son; or sometimes before the words of institution and after the anamnesis, thus manifesting the role of the Spirit in constituting the sacramental body of Christ and the ecclesial body.

These different places for the epiclesis correspond to different, though not contradictory, traditions which can co-exist peacefully within ecclesial unity.

It must be recognized, however, that the tendency of the Eastern liturgies is to stress the epiclesis, while making the words of institution simply a recitation and not a living, present word of consecration. The advantage of the Western tradition is that it unites the work of the Son and the work of the Spirit in the event of the eucharist.

The Holy Spirit makes the crucified and risen Christ really present for us in the eucharistic meal by fulfilling the promise contained in the words of institution of the Lord's supper. The role of the Holy Spirit in the eucharist is to make the historic words of Christ real and alive. It is not a matter of spiritualizing Christ's presence in the eucharist, but of affirming the indissoluble union of the Spirit and the Son. This union makes it clear that the eucharist is not a magical or mechanical act, but a prayer addressed to the Father, emphasizing the church's utter dependence upon him. In the assurance that its prayer will be granted because of Christ's promise in the words of institution, the church asks the Father to send down the Holy Spirit in order to accomplish the eucharistic event: the real presence of the crucified and risen Christ giving his life for all humanity. The words of institution, Christ's promise, and the epiclesis, the invocation of the Holy Spirit, are thus closely linked in the liturgy.

But the epiclesis is not solely for the consecration of the bread and the wine; it is also for the sanctification of the ordained minister and the community of the faithful. For the minister it is, in a sense, a renewal of ordination, and for the whole community a renewal of their baptism and confirmation. Here the Holy Spirit is the link uniting all the sacraments. We have lost the habit of kneeling at the consecration, and it is a pity. Would it not be appropriate for the celebrant to make a pause for silence before the epiclesis during which she or he stretches out his or her hands over the bread and the wine, to allow the congregation to kneel before the solemn invocation of the Holy Spirit? And the celebrant should pronounce the epiclesis of the Spirit and the words of Jesus slowly, uniting them in the one same moment of consecration.

The remembering of the gifts of the Spirit in the history of salvation is inspired by the liturgy of St James (4th century). The French Lutheran liturgy has also adopted this text (1977, variant VIII). The concept of the transfiguration of the eucharist by the Spirit originates with St Ambrose; it seeks to express the consecration of the bread and the wine in a mystical and sacramental mode which escapes our understanding and defies all explanation.

A sung response concludes the epiclesis: "Veni Creator Spiritus!" This punctuates the second part of the epiclesis, while the "Maranatha" marks the end of the anamnesis and the end of the commemorations.

Counting the *sanctus* and the acclamation after the words of institution, the eucharistic prayer is thus interrupted six times, greatly lightening this text which may often seem like a long prayed catechism. The short hymns sung by the congregation make the prayer more dynamic and easier to assimilate.

The link with the words of institution is made through the reference to the Creator Spirit who comes to fulfil the words of the beloved Son. Thus the union of the divine persons in the action of the eucharist is explicitly affirmed. Through the Spirit, the historical words of Jesus become real and effective and make the bread and the wine the body and blood of Christ: "The Spirit makes the crucified and risen Christ really present to us in the eucharistic meal, fulfilling the promise contained in the words of institution" (*BEM*, Eucharist, 14). The Holy Spirit "makes the historical words of Jesus present and alive" (Eucharist 14). The blessing of the bread and the cup is accompanied by thanksgiving, as in the Jewish liturgy, especially the Passover meal. The phrase "Do this for the remembrance of me" seeks to avoid the idea of mere memory, which is too subjective. The eucharist is a memorial, an anamnesis, that is, the event of salvation made actual, present once again. The anamnesis mentions the events of Christ's history, which are very much to the fore in the *BEM* document at this point. An important aspect of this anamnesis is the reference to Christ our Great High Priest interceding for all people with the Father in heaven. This is one of the important themes in *BEM*'s doctrine of the eucharist (Eucharist, 8).

The eucharist unites us with Christ the Intercessor and enables us, in communion with his unique priesthood, to present to the Father the anamnesis of the sacrifice of the cross. In fact, this anamnesis is not only the making actual of the unique event of Christ's sacrifice, it is also the substance of the church's offering, in the sense of the *azkarah* or *mnèmosynon* of biblical tradition; it is the *sacrifiium-memoriale*, through which the church remembers the sacrifice of the Son before the Father, that He may renew the grace of this unique sacrifice for it and for all human beings.

In the eucharist we are united with the unique priesthood of Christ in which all the people of God share, each according to his or her gifts and ministry. We offer the memorial of Christ, that is, we present the unique sacrifice of the Son before the Father as the church's ardent prayer and we say to God: "Remember the sacrifice of the cross and because of this unique sacrifice, source of all grace, grant to us, grant to all human beings the abundant blessings wrought for us by Christ's work of salvation and liberation". This is what the anamnesis or memorial means, making the unique sacrifice actual and present, and interceding that the Father may remember Christ's work on our behalf.

The eucharist, which the Father has given as a precious gift to his church, is received by him as intercession and thanksgiving, linked to the self-sacrifice of his Son who restored us into the covenant with God.

The second part of the epiclesis is inspired by the texts of the third and fourth Roman Catholic eucharistic prayer:

> *Respice, Domine, in Hostiam, quam Ecclesiae tuae ipse parasti (IV) et, agnoscens Hostiam, cuius voluisti immolatione placari, concede, ut qui Corpore et Sanguine Filii tui reficimur, Spiritu eius Sancto repleti, unum corpus et unus spiritus inveniamur in Christo (III), hostia viva ad laudem gloriae tuae (IV).*

This second part of the epiclesis calls for a fresh outpouring of the Spirit with the gift of the body and blood of Christ, so that the church may become one body and one spirit, a living sacrifice of praise to the Father. In the first epiclesis the Spirit is united with the Son to effect the eucharistic mystery; in the second they are united in the gift granted by the Father to his church so that it may be a sacrifice of praise to his glory.

As the church is assembled by the gift of the Spirit, it is only natural that the epiclesis should be followed by commemorations, remembering before God all the needs of church in the communion of saints and the hope of the kingdom to come. In this prayer of commemorations[4] we pray to God for the whole church, for its unity, its faith, its peace, for all its ministers, bishops, priests and deacons. We remember the faithful who have died, asking that they may be guided to the joyful feast prepared for all peoples, with Mary, the patriarchs and prophets, the apostles and martyrs. In Vancouver we recalled the memory of Maximilian Kolbe, Dietrich Bonhoeffer, Martin Luther King, Jr, Bishop Oscar Romero of San Salvador, Bishop Samuel of Egypt. The prayer ends on the vision of the kingdom where the whole creation is enabled to glorify the Father through the Son *(ubi cum universa creatura a corruptione peccati et mortis liberata, te glorificemus per Christum Dominum nostrum).*[5] Lastly, the grand conclusion spoken by the presiding minister ends with the solemn "Amen" of the whole congregation.

The prayers and hymns which accompany the communion (from the Lord's prayer to the post-communion) are classics of the Western liturgies. Only the thanksgiving prayer returns to the themes of *BEM*. We give thanks to God for having united us by baptism in the body of Christ and filling us with joy in the eucharist. We ask him to lead us towards the full visible unity of his church and to treasure all the signs of reconciliation already granted to us. The prayer of thanksgiving ends with the hope of the kingdom of which the eucharist has given us a foretaste, praying that "one day we may share in the inheritance of the saints in light" (Col. 1:12).

In 1520 Luther wrote these lines about the liturgy which will serve to summarize the meaning of the "Lima" liturgy:

It is not we who sacrifice Christ, but Christ who sacrifices us. In this way it is right, even useful, to call the mass a sacrifice, not in itself, but only that we sacrifice ourselves with Christ, that is to say that we rest on Christ with a firm faith in his testament and that we appear before God with our prayer, our praise and our sacrifice, only through him and his intermediacy... without doubting that he is our priest in heaven before God. Christ welcomes us, he presents us (to God), us, our prayer and our praise; he also sacrifices himself in heaven for us... he sacrifices himself in heaven for us and sacrifices us with him.[6]

NOTES

[1] *Baptism, Ministry and Eucharist*, Faith and Order paper no. 111, Geneva, WCC, 1982.

[2] B. Capelle, "Le kyrie de la messe et le pape Gélase", *Revue benedictine*, 1934, pp.136-38; A. Hammann, *Prières des premiers chrétiens*, Paris, Fayard, 1952, pp.349-52.

[3] *Fragment de Dêr-Balyzeh*, 6th century, witness to the liturgy of St Mark; *Quam oblationem* of the Roman canon and epicleses of the new eucharistic prayers. See my book *Le mystère eucharistique*, Paris, Centurion, 1981, pp.89-99.

[4] Cf. Consultation on Church Union, "Word, Bread and Cup", Cincinnati, Ohio, 1978.

[5] Roman Catholic eucharistic prayer IV.

[6] Weimar Edition VI, 369.

The Lima Liturgy and Beyond
Moving Forward Ecumenically

GORDON W. LATHROP

How can the eucharist indeed be the sacrament of unity? How can its celebration unite us rather than be the occasion for an intense and painful exhibition of our disunity? Yet how, at the same time, can its celebration always be truly local, the catholic church dwelling in this particular place, among these particular people where the celebration is held? And how can the profound structures of its unity also enable a real and welcomed diversity between us?

The urgency of these current ecumenical questions is sometimes heightened when, with this perspective in mind, we read ancient texts about the unity of Christian eucharistic practice amid an accepted diversity. For example, there is this famous text from a letter of Irenaeus, quoted in the *Ecclesiastical History* of Eusebius.[1] Irenaeus is urging the late 2nd-century bishop of Rome, Victor, not to cut off communion with the churches of Asia Minor. He asks Victor to remember that disagreement and difference in ritual matters (in this case, disagreement about when or even whether to observe pascha and its fast, the primitive Christian Easter) had not always led to breaking of communion. Here was a case in which thanksgiving at table and the rite of communion could still be shared.

> ... the presbyters before you who did not observe [the pascha] sent the eucharist to those from parishes who did. And when the blessed Polycarp [from Smyrna in Asia Minor] was staying at Rome in the time of Anicetus [in the mid-2nd century],... neither could Anicetus persuade Polycarp not to observe, seeing that he had always observed with John the disciple of our Lord and the rest of the apostles with whom he had passed his time, nor did Polycarp persuade Anicetus to observe, who said he was obligated to hold the customs of the presbyters who were before him. But with things in this state, they were in communion with each other, and in the church, Anicetus yielded the thanksgiving to Polycarp, with manifest respect, and they parted from each other in peace, all the church being in peace, both those who observed and those who did not observe.

According to Irenaeus, Polycarp and Anicetus were in communion across disagreement and a difference in tradition, even apostolic tradition. They shared a pattern: thanksgiving at table and the rite of communion. Or at least they shared enough of a deep and basic pattern as to enable Anicetus to yield the thanksgiving at table to Polycarp and to enable the communion to be sent.[2]

The Lima liturgy

On recent ecumenical occasions throughout the world, the so-called Lima liturgy[3] has provided a possible answer to these questions of communion amid diversity. What it has given us is not so much a pattern as an actual text. While the text of this liturgy has had no official standing in any church, it has had a growing history of ecumenical use. It became a place in which diverse churches could meet each other. In fact, the text had a quite specific origin which enabled the history of its use. Fine liturgy is always local, and the Lima liturgy was no exception. It was drafted by Frère Max Thurian for the 1982 meeting of the Faith and Order commission in Lima, Peru, the meeting at which the document *Baptism, Eucharist and Ministry* was adopted. It was drafted, as the texts of its prayers so frequently disclose, with the consensus of that document and the spirit of its drafting body quite clearly in mind. And it was further edited, by a small ecumenical committee, at the meeting for which it was intended. So the Lima meeting itself was the "local" origin of this liturgy.[4] From that meeting – and then from the use of the same liturgical text at the Vancouver assembly of the WCC in 1983 – other communities drew courage and interest for their own use and adaptation of the Lima liturgy. The excellence of the liturgical text, the history of its origin, and its resonance with widespread ecumenical experience all contributed to its wider use.

But the Lima liturgy had a local origin in another sense as well. Frère Max brought to the drafting task not only his participation in the Faith and Order work and his careful attention to the content of *BEM* dialogues. He also brought his years of experience in the formation of the liturgy of Taizé. In many ways, the Lima liturgy is the fruit of the local, ecumenical life of the community of Taizé. Its nearest textual neighbour is to be found in the eucharistic liturgy of Taizé,[5] and its widespread success is not unrelated to the respect and trust so generally accorded to the work of that community.

The text of the Lima liturgy thus represents a local liturgy – from Taizé and from several specific ecumenical gatherings and their common life – which spread more widely in its use, a text which allowed many churches to meet in mutual recognition and koinonia. Because of its origin in the work of these scholars and these monks, this text has become a kind of depository not only of ecumenical insights, but also of many of the fruits of 19th- and 20th-century liturgical studies and the liturgical movement.

One can, of course, criticize the liturgy of Lima.[6] The very liturgical studies that are represented so clearly in its conception might, for example, raise these questions: Can the diverse lay and ordained leadership roles, so important to Christian assembly, be more clearly indicated? Might the penitential rite be better placed before the entrance hymn or psalm rather than in the main body of the liturgy itself? Can the kyrie be used as a clear – and, perhaps, more extensive – litany of entrance? Can the collect function more strongly as the prayer of entrance? Can the text itself give some ecumenical attention to lectionary suggestions? Might hymnody play a more important role? Might there be alternate forms for intercessions with the possibility of free and local prayers included? Is the place of the peace in the communion rite really a good choice for ecumenical assemblies? Could the offertory prayers be eliminated, granted the presence of a strong *anaphora* and, therefore, the absence of the necessity of any further prayer over the gifts? Can the strongly thematic character of the prayer texts be avoided or reduced, yielding more attention to the always central yet perpetually changing theme of the scriptures of the day in relationship to our salvation in Christ? In general, could there be fewer words?

But while such questions may be raised and discussed, the liturgy cannot be criticized for not solving the deeper questions of mutual eucharistic sharing. This text gives the churches a possible place to meet. It does not resolve the ecclesial issue of mutual recognition of ministries. Its use does raise the fascinating question as to what a local church actually is. Is a gathering of people – perhaps even people from differing confessions and disciplines – who celebrate the eucharist together to be regarded as in some sense a "church"? Or what is the local church which holds the supper when an ecumenical assembly makes use of Lima? And who are the ministers, the liturgical leaders and servers who belong to the liturgical action, who rightly serve this local church? Still, while the use of the Lima liturgy does heighten these questions, a liturgical text itself cannot be expected to give answers.

Beyond the Lima liturgy

But there is a deeper criticism to be made of the Lima liturgy. Or rather, there is a trajectory of development which might rightly carry forward the work that Lima has begun. The very ecumenical liturgical studies and movement which have so significantly contributed to the Lima liturgy have also continued to develop. In fact, we might now speak of three matters that can claim a widespread scholarly consensus and that challenge ecumenical eucharistic celebrations to go beyond Lima. These matters are the nature of the shape of the eucharistic liturgy, the importance of liturgical inculturation, and the content of eucharistia at the table of the Lord. One might summarize these matters of widespread consensus in this way:

Shape: Liturgy is an event with a shape. It is more than a text. It is the flow of a communal action which expresses its meanings in gestures and concrete signs as well as in words. Indeed, the meanings of the liturgy come to expression by the continual juxtapositions of words with sign-actions. So the liturgy of the eucharist is made up of word-service set next to table-service in order to express the truth of Jesus Christ, in order to gather all people into the grace and life of the triune God. More, the eucharist's word-service sets scripture readings next to preaching and so leads the community to intercessory prayers. Its table-service sets eucharistia, thanksgiving at the table, next to eating and drinking the gift of Christ and so leads the community to mission. Around these central matters occur movements of gathering, collecting for the poor, and sending, significant in their juxtaposition to word and table. The whole action is done by a participating community together with its ministers, thus bringing to expression the body of Christ. And it is usually held on a Sunday or festival, juxtaposed to our "ordinary" days, so that Christian eschatology – the presence now of God's promised future for the cosmos – may be proclaimed. Such is the "shape of the liturgy".[7]

Inculturation: Liturgy is always celebrated locally. It goes together with a local church. It takes place in local speech, in the midst of the gifts and the problems of local cultures and traditions, reflecting its light on local needs. Inculturation of the liturgy is one of the oldest traditions of the church, found already in the making of the Christian sacraments out of the meals and washing rites of late-antique Judaism and continued in the extensive influence on Christian worship exerted by Hellenistic mysteries, imperial buildings and court rituals, and the adoption of new languages. And this inculturation must continue, in each new place, treasuring and transforming cultures new and old, dominant and threatened. Yet the universal character of the gospel of Christ and the very unity of the triune God also call every celebration to reflect the shared deep-pattern of the liturgy and the shared transcultural gifts of water, word and meal. It is astounding that these latter material things – always local gifts in their actual origin, yet always universal in human resonance and recognition – have been made into the bearers of the central Christian meanings and, by the promise of God and the power of the Spirit, of the very presence of Jesus Christ. Liturgy also is catholic, "universal".

Eucharistia: Thanksgiving at the table is made up of praise and beseeching, like all classic Christian prayer. In eucharistic praying, the praise has especially remembered the mighty deeds of God in the past, making memorial of the events of our salvation in the death and resurrection of Christ. The beseeching has especially asked for the presence and power of the Spirit, for the one who brings the promise of God's future into our own time and meeting, transfiguring this very assembly and meal. This great pattern of prayer at the table has been worked out in a variety of sub-patterns, some of them especially marked by different choices in the placement of the "institution narrative", the *verba institutionis*, of the supper of Christ. Outlined in large strokes, we can say that the Eastern, Antiochan sub-pattern places these *verba* in the "praise" part of the prayer, as a public proclamation and confession of the amazing gift of Christ, while letting the "beseeching" part of the prayer focus on the epiclesis of the Spirit. The Alexandrian and Roman sub-pattern, on the other hand, places the words of Christ at the supper in the beseeching part of the prayer, using these very words to beg God to fulfill the promise and gift of Christ now, and surrounding these words with the language-style of ancient Roman petitions to the emperor. In the Roman use, only a vestige of the epiclesis remains. Both patterns are legitimate developments. But the large number of modern eucharistic prayers throughout the world and in many churches have primarily been modelled on the Antiochan pattern. This may be so because of the perceived sense that the church needs to acknowledge its dependence on God by the use of a full epiclesis. It may also be so that the imperial language and the use of the *verba* in beseeching is simply not understandable today. Rather, the medieval misunderstanding perdures: placing the words of Christ in the Roman position, following a vestigial epiclesis, seems to indicate that the presider's recitation "confects" the sacrament and creates the presence of Christ.[8]

We do not know the pattern of Polycarp's thanksgiving at table,[9] but we can see that these contemporary matters of consensus do connect us with the ancient report of Irenaeus. It is not a text which unites Polycarp and Anicetus and their churches amid their disagreement and diversity; it is a shared pattern.

A way forward

One can see that these three matters of consensus are, in fact, represented in the Lima text itself. The Lima liturgy is marked by the very shape of the liturgy we have already discussed, although its character as text may obscure that fact. Furthermore, the Lima liturgy had a local origin and, encouraged by the drafter of the text himself,[10] continual adaptations of the text – and of its shape – have been made in new local situations. Even the eucharistia of the text, while modelled most strongly on the Roman pattern, has been influenced by the Antiochan use: the epiclesis is indeed before the *verba*, but it is by no means fragmentary or vestigial; it is a full, strong prayer for the power of the Spirit.

Still, these three matters press our experience of the Lima liturgy towards a further development. In truth, the text of Lima is experienced as just that, as text, not as pattern or shape. That fact limits its usefulness in new local situations, its accessibility to inculturation. And the *anaphora* of Lima does not represent the mainstream of rich, current ecumenical development in eucharistic praying, including the development in Roman Catholic circles, while it does run the risk of the medieval misunderstandings of "consecration".[11]

A way forward may be found in these two proposals: Take the *shape of the liturgy* as a profound ecumenical meeting place, as a basis for renewal, recognition and inculturation. And let there be an ecumenical exchange of the *current eucharistic prayers* of widespread usage and excellence, an exchange that allows the euchology of many churches to be echoed throughout the world.

There has been considerable recent ecumenical attention to the "shape of the liturgy" as an ordo of texts and actions.[12] Passages from the report of the Ditchingham consultation on koinonia in worship may stand as one summary of that attention:

> 4. The pattern of this gathering and sending has come to all the churches as a common and shared inheritance. That received pattern resides in the basic outlines of what may be called the *ordo* of Christian worship, i.e. the undergirding structure which is to be perceived in the ordering and scheduling of the most primary elements of Christian worship. This *ordo*, which is always marked by pairing and by mutually reinterpretative juxtapositions, roots in word and sacrament held together. It is scripture readings and preaching together, yielding intercessions; and, with these, it is eucharistia and eating and drinking together, yielding a collection for the poor and mission in the world. It is formation in faith and baptizing in water together, leading to participation in the life of the community. It is ministers and people, enacting these things, together. It is prayers through the days of the week and the Sunday assembly seen together; it is observances through the year and the annual common celebration of the Pascha together. Such is the inheritance of all the churches, founded in the New Testament, locally practised today, and attested to in the ancient sources of both the Christian East and the Christian West...
>
> 7. But the patterns of word and table, of catechetical formation and baptism, of Sunday and the week, of Pascha and the year, and of assembly and ministry around these things – the principal pairs of Christian liturgy – do give us a basis for a mutually encouraging conversation between the churches. Churches may rightly ask each other about the local inculturation of this *ordo*. They may call each other towards a maturation in the use of this pattern or a renewed clarification of its central characteristics or, even, towards a conversion to its use...
>
> 8. This pattern or *ordo* of Christian worship belongs most properly to each local church, that is, to "all in each place"... This same pattern or *ordo* of Christian wor-

ship is a major basis for the koinonia between local churches, a koinonia spanning both space and time, uniting churches of the New Testament times, of the sweep of Christian history and of the present oikoumene. Such a koinonia can only be enriched by those authentic forms of inculturation which the *ordo* may have taken in each local church, not diminished.[13]

In reflecting on these Ditchingham passages, we might note that the earliest full account of Christian Sunday worship which we possess, a passage at the conclusion of Justin Martyr's 2nd-century *Apology*, is itself the description of a patterned action, a kind of "ordo".[14] We might further note that the *Baptism, Eucharist and Ministry* document itself proposes a list of elements of eucharistic liturgy, arranged generally in the manner of the shape of the liturgy.[15] And we might especially look at the many churches and groups of churches which have made a liturgical outline the basis of the materials they have given to local congregations.[16] A widely accepted *ordo* (shape or pattern) for the eucharist can provide for both local inculturation and widespread ecumenical recognition. An *ordo* can provide us with a place to meet.

But recent proposals have also suggested that eucharistic praying, in whatever local form, follows a pattern.[17] And there have been many eucharistic prayers, from ancient sources – such as Hippolytus or Basil[18] – or from modern composition[19] which have been used by more than one church, across persistent formal divisions. Those who reflect on the future of ecumenical eucharistic celebration, or those who actually plan such events, should pay attention to these patterns and these prayers.

A proposal

It is, then, the proposal of this paper that the World Council of Churches should consider publishing an evolved form of the Lima liturgy which takes these considerations into view.[20] Such a publication would include a clarified form of the possible simplifications and adaptations which the Lima text itself has often undergone. Or, better, it would publish an agreed-upon form of the *ordo* for the eucharist, together with a series of alternate texts for use in that *ordo* or patterns for those major liturgical texts which might be developed locally. It might also include suggestions for lay and ordained leadership, for music, for space or environment and for the appropriate use of images and the arts. It would especially include that variety of eucharistic prayers which have already had a widespread ecumenical acceptance, including the prayer of Lima itself.

Such publication would not be "a liturgy", but the materials for the creation of a liturgy in a local place, a liturgy arising out of a local dialogue and a common commitment. It would make the ongoing fruits of the ecumenical liturgical movement available to local planners.

Such a publication would not solve the problems of ecumenical eucharistic sharing. But it might make the questions of our continuing disunity more poignant. It might help us to see something of those great patterns which Polycarp and Anicetus shared – but which also we share. It might invite us again to overcome our continuing divisions, being transformed by God's mercy into a richly diverse communion of churches, all of whom find koinonia in our Lord Jesus Christ through his gift of holy word and holy table.

NOTES

[1] Eusebius, *Ecclesiastical History*, 5:24:15-17.
[2] For one reading of the significance of this text for the relationship between the "shape of the liturgy" and the search for Christian unity, see Gordon Lathrop, "Koinonia and the Shape of the Liturgy", in *Studia Liturgica* and in *La Maison-Dieu* (see note 12).
[3] See Max Thurian, ed., *Ecumenical Perspectives on Baptism, Eucharist and Ministry*, Faith and Order paper no. 116, Geneva, WCC, 1983, pp.225-46.
[4] It would be fruitful to consider at greater length the sense in which this meeting, like many ecumenical meetings, had the character of "church".
[5] *Eucharistie à Taizé*, Taizé, 1972.
[6] See, for example, the friendly and helpful critique of Robert Gribben, "The 'Lima Liturgy' – an Ecumenical Liturgical Text", in *One in Christ*, 20, 3, 1984, pp.249-56. See also the report, appendix 1, in Thomas F. Best and Dagmar Heller, eds, *So We Believe, So We Pray: Towards Koinonia in Worship*, Faith and Order paper no. 171, Geneva, WCC, 1995, pp.22-24.
[7] For a discussion of "shape" and liturgical meaning, see further Gordon Lathrop, *Holy Things: A Liturgical Theology*, Minneapolis, Fortress, 1993. See also Lawrence A. Hoffman, *Beyond the Text: A Holistic Approach to Liturgy*, Bloomington, IN, Indiana UP, 1987.
[8] "Unfortunately, this pattern has several disadvantages. It neglects the stronger of the ancient traditions. It also interrupts the flow of the narration of the wonderful things God has accomplished in creation and in history. It fails to emphasize the basic helplessness or praying attitude of the assembly and thus fails to help avoid a 'magical' notion of the institution narrative. Finally, this pattern could rob the epiclesis of one of its greatest strengths, viz., the ability to underline the unity between 'consecration' and communion. The fact that this pattern continues to be imposed on Roman Catholic eucharistic prayers calls for serious reconsideration." John H. McKenna, "The Epiclesis Revisited", in Frank C. Senn, ed., *New Eucharistic Prayers: An Ecumenical Study of Their Development and Structure*, New York, Paulist, 1987, p.183 (cf. p. 159 below).
[9] Though his prayer at death, as given in *Martyrdom of Polycarp* 14, does show a pattern of praise and beseeching over a cup and may well disclose the ancient shape of eucharistia in Smyrna.
[10] See *Ecumenical Perspectives, op. cit.*, p.233.
[11] See note 9.
[12] The 15th international congress of the Societas Liturgica was held in Dublin, 14-19 August 1995, on the theme "The Future Shape of the Liturgy". The papers have been published in *La Maison-Dieu*, 204, 1995, 4, and *Studia Liturgica*, 26, 1, 1996.
[13] *So We Believe, So We Pray, op. cit.*, pp.6-8.
[14] Justin Martyr, 1 *Apology*, 67.
[15] *Baptism, Eucharist and Ministry*, Faith and Order paper no. 111, Geneva, WCC, 1982, Eucharist, 27.
[16] See, among many other examples, *Book of Common Prayer*, New York, 1979, pp.400-401; *Erneuerte Agende*, Hanover, 1990, pp.32,42; *Book of Common Worship*, Louisville, KY, Westminster John Knox, 1993, pp.33,46; and *With One Voice: A Lutheran Resource for Worship*, Minneapolis, Augsburg Fortress, 1995, pp.8-9.
[17] *Book of Common Prayer*, pp.404-405; *Book of Common Worship*, p.156.
[18] *Eucharistic Prayer of Hippolytus*, Washington, ICEL, 1983; cf. *Lutheran Book of Worship*, ministers ed., Minneapolis, Augsburg, 1978, p.226; *Book of Common Worship*, pp.150-51; *Eucharistic Prayer of Saint Basil*, Washington, ICEL, 1985; cf. *Book of Common Prayer*, pp.373-75; *Book of Common Worship*, pp.146-49.
[19] *Eucharistic Prayer A*, Washington, ICEL, 1986; cf. *Book of Common Worship*, pp. 142-45. See also "Eucharistic Prayer V", in *With One Voice*, leaders ed., Minneapolis, Augsburg Fortress, 1995, pp.63-64. This prayer is also forthcoming in the liturgical book of the United Church of Canada. Many other examples, internationally, could be educed.
[20] See also the suggestions in appendix 1, paras 5-6, in *So We Believe, So We Pray*, p.23.

Celebrations of the Eucharist in Ecumenical Contexts

A PROPOSAL

Meeting at the Ecumenical Institute at Bossey, Switzerland, 12-21 May 1995, Christians from different churches and confessions throughout the world have considered the growing phenomenon of celebrations of the eucharist in ecumenical contexts.

Those gathered together have given thanks to God for the wide influence of the Lima liturgy[1] in many churches and for the tentative further steps which these churches have sometimes taken in the spirit of the Lima liturgy and of the *Baptism, Eucharist and Ministry* document.[2] They have noted that celebrations of the eucharist have taken place at international ecumenical gatherings, at regional and local ecumenical events and in small ecumenical communities. They have noted that these celebrations have, in the spirit of the Lima liturgy, often moved beyond one liturgical tradition simply showing its historic or current forms to the assembled Christians, many of whom are from other traditions. Rather, there has emerged a challenging new form of ecumenical prayer arising from a concern to enable the present actual community to pray together, from a theological convergence emerging from many sources, from a continued and shared scholarly exploration of the liturgical heritage of Christians, and from an eagerness to see that heritage celebrated in ways appropriate to the dignity and gifts of specific human cultural contexts throughout the world.

A substantial number of us, liturgists, theologians and pastors, have considered this phenomenon in more detail. Under discipline from the larger group, and in continuing discussion with it, we have felt moved to propose, on our own initiative and responsibility, the following pattern and guidelines to anyone engaged in planning eucharistic worship in an ecumenical context. In making this proposal, we have been helped especially by three classic texts important to the eucharist:

1) the account in Luke 24:13-35 of the risen Christ transforming two despairing disciples and sending them on mission by means of his living interpretation of the scriptures and his presence in the breaking of bread;

2) the 2nd-century account of Justin Martyr (1 *Apology,* 67) of the shape of the ancient eucharist on Sunday as including gathering, scripture reading, preaching, interceding, setting out the food, giving thanks, eating and drinking, sending to the absent and collecting for the poor;

3) the late 2nd-century report of Irenaeus of Lyon concerning the time when, in order to show unity, Anicetus, bishop of Rome, "yielded the thanksgiving" at the eucharistic table in the Roman church to Polycarp, the bishop of Smyrna (Eusebius, *Ecclesiastical History*, 5:24:11-18).

We have also been helped significantly by two of the widespread and growing fruits of the ecumenical movement: the *liturgical* convergence on a common pattern of eucharistic celebration reflected in the worship life of many churches, and the *theological* convergence on the meaning and grace of the eucharist represented by the Eucharist section of *BEM*.[3]

What follows are suggestions, offered in a spirit of love and prayer, which we present for consideration by those contemplating the celebration of a eucharist in an ecumenical context. None of these are intended to criticize the liturgies of participating churches or the liturgical traditions of denominations, confessions or communions. They come, rather, as a strong, descriptive proposal in order to urge planners not to forget the spirit of the Lima liturgy: a liturgical celebration recognizable to all, which nonetheless calls us all beyond our own experience to a wider unity.

We have found in the pattern of eucharistic worship we here present, and in our varied celebrations of this pattern, a witness to the historic catholic faith. We have also encountered therein a simple form of celebration which may be carried out in a rich variety of ways, which responds to the needs of the world in the present time, and which is capable of inculturation in many places. This basic pattern *(ordo)* is found on page 35 below. It is consistent with the listing given in *BEM*;[4] but our presentation seeks to show the inherent simplicity and clarity of the eucharistic service, to reveal its underlying structure, to make plain which parts are essential (and which optional), and to suggest both the movement and flow of the service as a whole, and the dynamic relationships among its parts.

We have also found that these discoveries lead us to important conclusions regarding Christian unity. For example, we are well aware that it is often primarily questions of ministry and authority which prevent Christians from coming together at the table of the Lord. We are well aware of the complexity and sensitivity of the issues involved. And yet we continue to wonder whether the churches, on the basis of the acceptance of this pattern by all participating communions, might be prepared to extend to each other an "interim eucharistic hospitality" (that is, the giving of an invitation for all present at an event to receive communion), at least for major ecumenical gatherings.

But whatever answer might be given to this question, we would ask any group of Christians planning eucharistic worship in an ecumenical context to consider these questions with us:

1. Do you recognize this liturgical pattern as bearing the historic catholic faith which unites your church to the other Christian churches?
2. Do you recognize this liturgical pattern as bearing the world in which we live, as showing forth its conditions plainly, and proclaiming its transformation in Christ?
3. If so, what implications flow from these recognitions?

In order to aid your planning and to give a basis for these questions we share with you the following convictions. They are intended to be read in conjunction with the pattern *(ordo)* for eucharistic worship given on page 35 below.

1. A celebration of the eucharist in an ecumenical context includes a clear service of the word and a clear service of the table.

This event of word and table should be preceded by a holy gathering of the assembly into the grace, love and koinonia of the triune God and followed by an appropriate sending of the assembly in witness and service. In regard to this gathering and sending, see paragraphs 7 and 8 below.

2. The service of the word in such a eucharist includes two clear components: scripture reading *from the Old and the New Testaments, and* proclamation *of the crucified and risen Jesus Christ as the source and ground of our life in God's grace. Readings and preaching together should then lead the assembly to a response to the word in intercessions for the need of the world and for the unity of the church, confession of the faith, and song.*

The confession of the faith should occur, either here, after the sermon, or in preparation for the service of the table, in the original text of the Nicene Creed (Constantinople 381 CE), as that text which expresses the widest measure of doctrinal consensus amongst the churches.

A collection for people in need or in support of an agreed cause may also be an appropriate response at this point, associated with the intercessions, or it may occur at the end of the service of the table.

Biblical texts should be carefully chosen with respect to the occasion and with attention to the various lectionaries represented in the participating churches.

The proclamation of Christ will ordinarily take the form of a prepared sermon. In smaller groups, it may also involve the preacher engaging the assembly in active reflection on the word.

The service of the word may also include other elements which respond to and support these components, for example, meditating on the word in silence, the singing of hymns and contemporary songs, the singing of psalms; the singing of the classic short hymns appropriate to a feast day *(kontakia)* and the hymns or antiphons made up of psalm verses which may accompany a scripture reading *(prokeimena)*, and other such liturgical elements of the Eastern traditions; or alleluia verses and sequences and other such liturgical elements of the Western tradition. The exchange of the peace may conclude and seal the intercessions and prepare for the service of the table.

3. The service of the table in such a eucharist includes two clear components: a thanksgiving *at table, and the communal* eating and drinking *of the bread and cup of the thanksgiving, the holy gifts of Jesus Christ's living and active presence. Thanksgiving and communion together should then lead the assembly to mission.*

The thanksgiving should include the historic dialogue *(sursum corda)*, praise to God for creation and redemption, the words of Christ at the institution of the supper, the explicit memorial (anamnesis) of the passion, death and resurrection of Jesus Christ, the explicit prayer for the coming day of God, expressed in invocation of the Holy Spirit (epiclesis) and commemorations, the "amen" of the entire assembly, and the Lord's prayer. This thanksgiving is best proclaimed with frequent responses from the entire assembly.

The use of a single loaf of bread and a large single cup should be seriously considered.

The collection for those in need may also occur at the end of the service of the table, but it ought not to be omitted nor should it be used for ecclesiastical expenses nor for the costs of the event. It may consist of gifts of food for the hungry.

The service of the table may also include a ceremonial presentation of gifts, an invitation to communion, and the singing of classic or modern communion songs.

4. The entire event of such a eucharist should be musical, with the great structure of the assembly's action unfolded in the culturally diverse song and movement of the churches of the world.

That music – and the space of the liturgy together with its visual arts – should serve the essential flow of the structure of the rite, not obscure it. It should engage the assembly in that flow. For example, great care needs to be exercised in the choice of such words in hymnody and song as most clearly express the shared catholic faith, the scripture readings of the celebration, their place in the order, the sense of the Sunday or festival, and the unity of the church.

The sharing of our different heritages of music, our creativity, and the exploration of our cultures have made a vital contribution to ecumenical worship over recent years. We have learned that every culture has a rich gift to bring to worship, and that worship may be enhanced by many musical styles and rhythms, chosen with care and sensitivity to their liturgical function.

5. The celebration of such a eucharist involves a participating assembly and many liturgical ministries. Its unity is best served by one person presiding, in order to serve the unity and flow of the whole liturgy and to draw forth the gifts present in the assembly.

A celebration of the eucharist in an ecumenical context should, as far as possible, while respecting ecclesial disciplines, involve the active participation of all the assembly. The planning should involve members, both ordained and lay, of all the traditions represented. It should also involve the liturgical ministry of both lay and ordained Christians in reading, singing and leading song, praying, dancing, serving and gathering.

A single ordained pastor, presbyter or bishop, whose ministry is recognized in a participant church, should preside. "In order to fulfil its mission, the church needs persons who are publicly and continually responsible for pointing to its fundamental dependence on Jesus Christ, and thereby provide, within a multiplicity of gifts, a focus of its unity."[5] Careful reflection should be given to this leadership. The presider may come from the leadership of a local host church. Ordinarily the presider will greet the assembly, preach, proclaim the thanksgiving and bless the assembly as they are sent. Presiding may sometimes take the form of the presider yielding place to another preacher or to another leader of the eucharistic prayer. "Concelebration", understood as group presidency by ordained ministers from different confessions, raises more ecumenical problems than it solves.

The ministers, lay and ordained, who lead this service could each be clothed in a garment which may be recognized as proclaiming our common baptism into Christ and as representing the entire assembly. Other signs of festivity or service, drawn from the historic Christian vestments or the current cultures of the churches, may mark the principal ministers, especially the presider.

6. *In planning such a celebration of the eucharist, consideration should be given to holding the celebration on a Sunday or other Christian festival as a sign of the mystery of the resurrection that unites us.*

In many places in the world, the special sense of Sunday needs to be recovered. The Lord's supper belongs first of all to the Lord's day. Furthermore, ecumenism is central, not peripheral, to the life of the churches. This is not intended to preclude the choice of other days when Sunday or festivals are not practicable for a particular ecumenical event.

7. *The gathering may include various actions, but it should draw the assembly, bearing in itself the need and longings of the world and the reality of each local place, into the grace and mercy of God.*

Such a gathering is based upon our common baptism into the mystery of the triune God and so into the church. This gathering may include singing the praise of God, confession and forgiveness or some other baptismal remembrance, a call to worship or biblical greeting, a kyrie or litany of entrance, gloria in excelsis or other doxology, and a traditional collect or prayer of entrance. It is not suggested that all of these ways of gathering should be used, nor that more possibilities should be planned for a large event or fewer for a small: but people in each place need to ask how gathering in the grace and mercy of God can take place appropriately *here*, reflecting local cultural customs.

8. *The dismissal may include various actions, but it should send the assembly to serve in love and to bear witness to the freedom of life in Christ, and to the justice, peace and integrity of creation willed by God.*

The dismissal will receive and enact all the ways in which the liturgy has stirred the assembly to action. It may be marked by a post-communion prayer committing the communicants to the mission of Christ, by singing, a blessing on departure, a word of dismissal, the possible sending of the holy communion or other gifts to those who are absent, or the sending of food to the poor.

9. *Participation in the proclaimed word and the prayers of the assembly is participation in Christ. It is also Christ who, in the power of the Spirit, invites all to eat and drink his holy gift.*

Nonetheless, participants in the liturgy who are not able to receive communion at all, or not able to receive one or the other of the holy gifts, should not be shamed or made to feel unwelcome. They should be encouraged to participate as far as they are able, to behold in love and adoration Christ who gives himself to these others of his people, to understand themselves as belonging through baptism to Christ as well, and to pray for the day of fuller Christian unity.

10. *The extensive options listed here ought not obscure the simple order proposed: this liturgy could be celebrated with great simplicity or with extensive local experiment toward an emerging pattern of the future.*

The pattern is quite simple (see the *ordo* on page 35). And, granted a clear word and table structure, local ecumenical groups are encouraged to discover how this great gift of God might be newly and faithfully unfolded. A simple service, however, should not omit the central elements of Christ's gift nor should an elaborate or experimental service obscure them.

11. As a liturgy is prepared according to these proposals, texts for the principal parts of the eucharist may best be chosen from prayers which have been accorded a wide ecumenical reception.

In the selection of texts for the liturgy, including the scripture version to be used, careful attention should be given to the use of inclusive language. Different cultures will call for different solutions, but the goal is always to find language which will include as many as possible in full participation in the prayer.

Following the interim guidelines for the Canberra assembly of the World Council of Churches,[6] biblical language and significant traditional formulas should be preserved.

NOTES

[1] "The Eucharistic Liturgy: Liturgical Expression of Convergence in Faith Achieved in *Baptism, Eucharist and Ministry*", Geneva, WCC, 1983; a reprint of "The Eucharistic Liturgy of Lima", *Ecumenical Perspectives on Baptism, Eucharist and Ministry*, Max Thurian, ed., Faith and Order paper no. 116, Geneva, WCC, 1983, pp.225-46. The Lima liturgy, an unofficial text of the Faith and Order commission, was developed to express in liturgical form the theological convergences reached in the official *Baptism, Eucharist and Ministry* document.

[2] Faith and Order paper no. 111, Geneva, WCC, 1982.

[3] *Ibid.*, pp.9-17.

[4] Eucharist, 27, pp.15-16.

[5] *Ibid.*, Ministry, 8, p.21.

[6] See Per Harling, ed., *Worshipping Ecumenically: Orders of Service from Global Meetings with Suggestions for Local Use*, Geneva, WCC, 1995, pp.3-4.

The Fundamental Pattern *(Ordo)* of the Eucharistic Service

GATHERING of the assembly into the grace, love and koinonia of the triune God

WORD-SERVICE

Reading of the scriptures of the Old and New Testaments

Proclaiming Jesus Christ crucified and risen as the ground of our hope

(and confessing and singing our faith)

and so *interceding* for all in need and for unity

(sharing the peace to seal our prayers and prepare for the table)

TABLE-SERVICE

Giving thanks over bread and cup

Eating and drinking the holy gifts of Christ's presence

(collecting for all in need)

and so

BEING SENT (DISMISSAL) in mission in the world

The following were members of the group which developed this text:

Rev. Robert Gribben (United)
Rev. Dennis Hughes (Presbyterian)
Fr Brian Jemmot (Anglican)
Pastor Gerd Kerl (United)
Rev. Gordon Lathrop (Lutheran)
Rev. Jaci Maraschin (Anglican)
Mrs Joan Matthews (Baptist)
Rev. Rodney Matthews (Baptist)
Rev. Thomas Best (Disciples of Christ)
Rev. Janet Crawford (Anglican)
Rev. Dagmar Heller (United)

In addition, our general discussion was enriched by Fr Elias Thandikayil (Oriental Orthodox), who was able to be present during many of our sessions.

Eucharistiefeiern

bei ökumenischen Zusammenkünften

EIN VORSCHLAG

Eine Gruppe von Christen aus verschiedenen Kirchen und Konfessionen aus der ganzen Welt, die vom 12.-21. Mai 1995 im Ökumenischen Institut Bossey/Schweiz zu einem Seminar zusammenkam, beschäftigte sich mit dem immer häufiger auftretenden Phänomen von Eucharistiefeiern in ökumenischen Zusammenhängen.

Dabei wurde Freude und Dankbarkeit darüber zum Ausdruck gebracht, dass die Lima-Liturgie[1] von vielen Kirchen aufgenommen wurde und vorsichtige weitere Schritte im Geiste der Lima-Liturgie und des Limatextes[2] unternommen worden sind. Es wurde zur Kenntnis genommen, dass Eucharistiefeiern sowohl auf internationalen ökumenischen Tagungen, bei regionalen und lokalen ökumenischen Veranstaltungen wie auch in kleinen ökumenischen Gemeinschaften stattfinden. Ebenfalls nahm man zur Kenntnis, dass diese Feiern – im Geiste der Lima-Liturgie – oft über eine bestimmte liturgische Tradition hinausgehen, indem sie nicht einfach nur den versammelten Christen, von denen viele aus anderen Traditionen kommen, ihre historischen oder gegenwärtigen Formen zeigen. Aus dem Anliegen heraus, das gemeinsame Beten einer konkreten Gemeinschaft möglich zu machen, aber auch aus einer theologischen Konvergenz heraus, die sich aus vielen Quellen nährt, ist vielmehr eine herausfordernde neue Form ökumenischen Gebets entstanden. Dazu hat aber auch die ständige gemeinsame wissenschaftliche Erforschung des liturgischen christlichen Erbes beigetragen sowie das Bestreben, dieses Erbe in der ganzen Welt auf eine Art und Weise gefeiert zu sehen, die der Würde und den Gaben konkreter kultureller Kontexte angemessen sind.

Während des zweiten Teils der Tagung teilten sich die Teilnehmer in verschiedene Arbeitsgruppen auf. Eine davon, bestehend aus Liturgiewissenschaftler/innen, Theolog/innen und Pfarrer/innen hat sich mit diesem Phänomen genauer beschäftigt und folgenden Text verfasst:

In Verbindung mit der gesamten Gruppe und in ständigem Austausch mit ihr fühlten wir uns veranlasst, auf eigene Initiative und Verantwortung all denjenigen, die eucharistische Gottesdienste bei ökumenischen Zusammenkünften vorbereiten, die nachfolgenden Richtlinien zur Gestaltung sowie ein Grundmodell für solche Gottesdienste vorzuschlagen. Dabei waren drei klassische Texte, die für das Thema Eucharistie wichtig sind, besonders hilfreich:

• Übersetzt aus dem Englischen von Dagmar Heller und Renate Sbeghen.

1. Die Erzählung vom auferstandenen Christus, der zwei zweifelnde Jünger aufrichtet und durch seine lebendige Auslegung der Schrift wie durch seine Gegenwart beim Brotbrechen zur Verkündigung aussendet (Lk 24,13-35).
2. Die Darstellung der Gestalt der frühen sonntäglichen Eucharistiefeier bei Justin dem Märtyrer aus dem 2. Jahrhundert (1 Apologie 67). Dort werden folgende Elemente aufgeführt: Sich-Versammeln, Lesen der Schrift, Predigen, Fürbitte halten, die Gaben darbringen, Dank sagen, Essen und Trinken, Aussenden zu den Abwesenden und das Sammeln für die Armen.
3. Der Bericht des Irenäus von Lyon aus dem späten zweiten Jahrhundert, der sich auf die Zeit bezieht, als Anicletus, Bischof von Rom, um die Einheit sichtbar zu machen, Polykarp, dem Bischof von Smyrna "die Danksagung" am eucharistischen Tisch "überliess" (Euseb, Kirchengeschichte, 5,24,11-18).

Ausserdem halfen uns in bezeichnender Weise zwei der weitverbreiteten und wachsenden Früchte der ökumenischen Bewegung: die *liturgische* Konvergenz über ein gemeinsames Modell eucharistischer Feier, wie es sich im gottesdienstlichen Leben vieler Kirchen abzeichnet, und die *theologische* Konvergenz über Bedeutung und Eigenschaft der Eucharistie, wie sie im Abschnitt über die Eucharistie in "Taufe, Eucharistie und Amt" dargestellt ist.[3]

Im folgenden werden – im Geist der Nächstenliebe und des Gebets – Anregungen angeboten, die wir all denen zur Überlegung vorlegen, die über die Eucharistiefeier in ökumenischen Zusammenhängen nachdenken. Keiner dieser Vorschläge will die Liturgien beteiligter Kirchen oder die liturgischen Traditionen von Denominationen, Konfessionen oder Gemeinschaften kritisieren. Sie sind vielmehr gedacht als ein überzeugender, anschaulicher Vorschlag, um bei der Vorbereitung den Geist der Lima-Liturgie nicht zu vergessen: eine Eucharistiefeier in ökumenischem Kontext ist eine liturgische Feier, die für alle als solche erkennbar ist und uns gleichzeitig über unsere eigene Erfahrung hinaus zu weitergehender Einheit ruft.

Im Modell des eucharistischen Gottesdienstes, das wir hier vorlegen und in verschiedenen Feiern dieses Modells, die hier in Bossey stattgefunden haben, haben wir ein Zeugnis des historischen katholischen Glaubens gefunden. Wir sind darin auch auf eine einfache Form der Feier gestossen, die in einer reichen Formenvielfalt gefeiert werden kann und auf die Bedürfnisse der Welt in der heutigen Zeit eingeht sowie zur Inkulturation an vielen Orten fähig ist. Dieses Grundmodell (ordo) findet sich auf Seite 43 unten. Es stimmt überein mit der Auflistung in "Taufe, Eucharistie und Amt",[4] aber unsere Darstellung versucht, die dem eucharistischen Gottesdienst innewohnende Einfachheit und Klarheit aufzuzeigen und die ihm zugrunde liegende Struktur zu enthüllen. Sie will klarmachen, welche Teile wesentlich (und welche freigestellt) sind, und sowohl die innere Bewegung als auch den äusseren Ablauf des Gottesdienstes als ganzes wie auch die dynamische Beziehung zwischen den einzelnen Teilen andeuten.

Wir waren auch der Meinung, dass diese Entdeckungen zu wichtigen Schlussfolgerungen im Blick auf die Einheit der Christen führen. Zum Beispiel: Wir sind uns dessen wohl bewusst, dass es oft hauptsächlich Fragen des Amtes und der Autorität sind, die Christen daran hindern, sich gemeinsam am Tisch des Herrn zu versammeln. Wir sind uns wohl der Komplexität und der Sensibilität der damit zusammenhängenden Problemkreise bewusst. Und doch fragen wir uns immer wieder, ob die Kirchen auf der Grundlage, dass dieses Modell von allen teilnehmenden Gemeinschaften akzeptiert wird, vielleicht bereit wären, einander "vorläufige eucharistische Gastfreundschaft" zu gewähren (gemeint ist, dass sie alle Anwesenden bei einem Gottesdienst einladen, das Abendmahl zu empfangen), wenigstens für grössere ökumenische Zusammenkünfte.

Aber welche Antwort diese Frage auch finden wird, möchten wir doch jede christliche Gruppe, die eucharistische Gottesdienste vorbereitet, bitten, folgende Fragen mit uns zu bedenken:

1. Können Sie dieses liturgische Modell erkennen als eines, das den historischen katholischen Glauben in sich trägt, der Ihre Kirche mit anderen christlichen Kirchen vereint?
2. Können Sie erkennen, dass dieses liturgische Modell die Welt in sich trägt, in der wir leben? Dass es ihre Bedingungen klar aufzeigt und ihre Veränderung in Christus verkündet?
3. Falls ja, welche Folgerungen ergeben sich aus diesen Erkenntnissen?

Wir möchten Ihnen im folgenden unsere Überzeugungen zur Hilfe bei der Vorbereitung und als Grundlage für diese Fragen an die Hand geben. Sie sind so gedacht, dass sie in Verbindung mit dem Modell (ordo) für den eucharistischen Gottesdienst auf S. 43 gelesen werden.

1. Eine Eucharistiefeier in einem ökumenischen Kontext besteht aus einem deutlich erkennbaren Wortteil *und einem deutlich erkennbaren* Abendmahlteil.

Diesen beiden Teilen sollte ein ehrfürchtiges Sich-Sammeln der Gemeinde in die Gnade, Liebe und Koinonia des dreieinigen Gottes vorangehen. Am Ende sollte eine angemessene Sendung der Gemeinde in Zeugnis und Dienst folgen. Zu diesem Sich-Sammeln und Senden vgl. Par. 7 und 8.

2. Der Wortteil in solch einer Eucharistiefeier besteht aus zwei deutlich erkennbaren Elementen: Lesung *aus dem Alten und Neuen Testament und* Verkündigung *des gekreuzigten und auferstandenen Christus als Quelle und Grund unseres Lebens in Gottes Gnade. Lesungen und Predigt zusammen sollten dann die Gemeinde zu einer Antwort auf das Gehörte führen, die sich in der Fürbitte für die Notleidenden der Welt und für die Einheit der Kirchen, im Glaubensbekenntnis und im Gesang ausdrückt.*

Das Glaubensbekenntnis sollte entweder hier, nach der Predigt, stehen oder in der Vorbereitung auf den Abendmahlteil, und zwar im ursprünglichen Text des Nizänischen Glaubensbekenntnisses (Konstantinopel 381) als dem Text, der das weitestgehende Mass lehrmässiger Übereinstimmung unter den Kirchen zum Ausdruck bringt.

Eine Sammlung für die Notleidenden oder für die Unterstützung eines vereinbarten Projekts verbunden mit den Fürbitten an dieser Stelle kann ebenfalls eine angemessene Antwort sein, wenn sie nicht am Ende des Mahlteiles durchgeführt wird.

Biblische Texte sollten mit Rücksicht auf den Anlass und mit Rücksicht auf die verschiedenen Lektionarien der verschiedenen teilnehmenden Kirchen sorgfältig ausgesucht werden.

Die Verkündigung Christi wird normalerweise in Form einer vorbereiteten Predigt stattfinden. In kleineren Gruppen kann der/die Prediger/in auch die versammelte Gemeinde in das aktive Nachdenken über das Wort mit hineinnehmen.

Der Wortteil kann auch andere Elemente mit einschliessen, die diesen Bestandteilen entsprechen und sie unterstützen und entfalten, wie z.B. eine stille Meditation über dem Wort, das Singen von traditionellen und zeitgenössischen Liedern, das Singen von Psalmen oder klassischen kurzen Gesängen, die sich auf einen Festtag beziehen *(Kontakia)* und Hymnen oder Antiphonen, die aus Psalmversen zusammengesetzt sind und die Schriftlesungen begleiten *(Prokeimena)* und andere derartige liturgische Elemente der östlichen Traditionen, oder Halleluja-Verse und Sequenzen und andere derartige Elemente aus der westlichen Tradition. Das Austauschen des Friedensgrusses kann die Fürbitten beschliessen und besiegeln sowie zum Abendmahlsteil überleiten.

3. Der Abendmahlsteil in solch einer Eucharistiefeier hat zwei klare Bestandteile: eine Danksagung *am Tisch und gemeinsames* Essen *des Brotes und Trinken aus dem Becher der Danksagung, der heiligen Gaben der lebendigen und aktiven Anwesenheit Jesu Christi. Danksagung und Austeilung zusammen sollten dann zur Sendung der Gemeinde hinführen.*

Die Danksagung sollte den historischen Dialog (sursum corda) beinhalten, den Lobpreis Gottes für die Schöpfung und Erlösung, die Worte Christi bei der Einsetzung des Abendmahles, die ausdrückliche Erinnerung (anamnesis) an das Leiden, den Tod und die Auferstehung Jesu Christi, das ausdrückliche Gebet für den Tag Gottes, an dem wir sein Kommen erwarten, ausgedrückt in der Anrufung des Heiligen Geistes (epiclesis) und den Gedächtnisbitten, das "Amen" der gesamten Gemeinde und das Vaterunser. Diese Danksagung kommt am besten zum Ausdruck, wenn die ganze Gemeinde mit häufigen Antworten beteiligt wird.

Die Verwendung eines einzigen Brotlaibs und eines einzigen grossen Kelchs sollte ernsthaft in Betracht gezogen werden.

Die Sammlung für die Notleidenden kann auch am Ende des Mahlteiles stattfinden, aber sie sollte nicht fehlen und auch nicht für kirchliche Ausgaben oder die Kosten der Veranstaltung verwendet werden. Sie kann auch aus Naturalien für die Hungernden bestehen.

Der Abendmahlsteil kann ausserdem eine feierliche Darbringung der Gaben, eine Einladung zur Kommunion und das Singen von klassischen oder modernen Kommuniongesängen mit einschliessen.

4. Der gesamte Ablauf einer solchen Eucharistiefeier sollte musikalisch begleitet werden, wobei die Gesamtstruktur des Handelns der Gemeinde in den kulturell unterschiedlichen Gesängen und Bewegungen der Kirchen in der ganzen Welt entfaltet wird.

Diese Musik – und der liturgische Raum zusammen mit seiner künstlerischen Ausgestaltung – sollte dem wesentlichen strukturellen Ablauf des Ritus dienen und ihn nicht verdunkeln. Sie sollte die versammelte Gemeinde in diesen Ablauf mit hineinnehmen. Z.B. muss grosse Sorgfalt auf die Auswahl von Worten verwendet werden, die den gemeinsamen katholischen Glauben, die Schriftlesungen in der Feier, ihren Platz im Ablauf, die Bedeutung des Sonntags oder Festes und die Einheit der Kirche zum Ausdruck bringen.

Der Austausch unseres unterschiedlichen musikalischen Erbes, unsere Kreativität und die Erforschung unserer Kulturen haben in den vergangenen Jahren einen wesentlichen Beitrag zur Gestaltung ökumenischer Gottesdienste geleistet. Wir haben gelernt, dass jede Kultur reiche Gaben in den Gottesdienst einbringen kann und dass er durch viele musikalische Stile und Rhythmen bereichert werden kann, wenn sie mit Sorgfalt und Feingefühl im Blick auf ihre liturgische Funktion ausgewählt werden.

5. Solch eine Eucharistiefeier schliesst eine teilnehmende Gemeinde ein und viele liturgische Ämter. Ihrer Einheit ist am besten gedient, wenn eine Person den Vorsitz hat, um der Einheit und dem Ablauf der ganzen Liturgie zu dienen und die in der Gemeinde vorhandenen Gaben zum Einsatz zu bringen.

Eine Eucharistiefeier in ökumenischem Kontext sollte so weit wie möglich die aktive Beteiligung der ganzen Gemeinde einschliessen, wobei kirchliche Regelungen respektiert werden. In die Vorbereitung sollten Vertreter aller repräsentierten Traditionen, sowohl Ordinierte als auch Laien, einbezogen werden. Das liturgische Amt von Laien wie Ordinierten sollte ebenso beim Lesen, Singen und Leiten des Gesangs, beim Beten, Tanzen, Dienen und Sich-Sammeln einbezogen werden.

Ein/e einzige/r ordinierte/r Geistliche/r, Presbyter/in oder Bischof/Bischöfin, dessen/deren Amt in einer der beteiligten Kirchen anerkannt wird, sollte den Vorsitz führen. "Um ihre Sendung zu erfüllen, braucht die Kirche Personen, die öffentlich und ständig dafür veranwortlich sind, auf ihre fundamentale Abhängigkeit von Jesus Christus hinzuweisen, und die dadurch innerhalb der vielfältigen Gaben einen Bezugspunkt ihrer Einheit darstellen."[5] Diese Leitungsaufgabe sollte sorgfältig durchdacht werden. Der/die Vorsitzende kann aus der Leitung einer örtlichen gastgebenden Kirche kommen. Normalerweise wird der/die Vorsitzende die Gemeinde begrüssen, die Predigt halten, die Danksagung beten und die Gemeinde bei der Sendung segnen. Den Vorsitz zu führen kann manchmal auch heissen, einem/r anderen Prediger/in den Platz zu überlassen oder jemandem anderen die Leitung des eucharistischen Gebets zu übergeben. "Konzelebration" im Sinne des gemeinsamen Vorsitzes einer Gruppe von ordinierten Amtsträgern aus verschiedenen Konfessionen schafft mehr ökumenische Probleme als dass sie zur Lösung beiträgt.

Die Amtsträger, Laien und Ordinierte, die diesen Gottesdienst leiten, können liturgische Gewänder tragen, die unsere gemeinsame Taufe in Christus symbolisieren und durch die die ganze Gemeinde repräsentiert wird. Auch andere Zeichen der Festlichkeit oder des Dienstes, die von den historischen christlichen Gewändern oder aus den gegenwärtigen Kulturen der Kirchen übernommen sind, können die leitenden Pfarrer und Pfarrerinnen, besonders die Person, die den Vorsitz innehat, kennzeichnen.

6. Bei der Planung einer solchen Eucharistiefeier sollte darauf geachtet werden, dass die Feier an einem Sonntag oder an einem anderen christlichen Festtag stattfindet als Zeichen des Geheimnisses der Auferstehung, das uns vereint.

An vielen Orten in der Welt muss die besondere Bedeutung des Sonntags wiedergewonnen werden. Das Abendmahl gehört zuallererst dem Tag des Herrn. Darüber hinaus gehört die Ökumene ins Zentrum und nicht an den Rand des kirchlichen Lebens. Das soll nicht heissen, dass die Wahl anderer Tage ausgeschlossen ist, wenn ein spezielles ökumenisches Ereignis nicht an einem Sonn- oder Feiertag durchführbar ist.

7. Das Sich-Sammeln kann verschiedene Handlungen beinhalten, aber es sollte die Gemeinde, die in sich die Bedürfnisse und Sehnsüchte der Welt wie auch die Realität jedes Ortes trägt, in die Gnade und Barmherzigkeit Gottes hineinführen.

Solches Sich-Sammeln gründet auf unserer gemeinsamen Taufe in das Mysterium des Dreieinigen Gottes und somit in die Kirche. Dieses Sich-Sammeln kann das Singen des Lobes Gottes einschliessen, ein Sündenbekenntnis und den Zuspruch der Vergebung oder eine andere Tauferinnerung, einen Aufruf zur Andacht oder Bibelverse zur Begrüssung, ein Kyrie oder eine Eingangslitanei, Gloria in excelsis oder eine andere Doxologie, und ein traditionelles Kollekten- oder Eingangsgebet. Es ist nicht vorgesehen, dass all diese Möglichkeiten des Sich-Sammelns vorkommen. Ebensowenig ist gemeint, dass bei einer grösseren Veranstaltung mehr Elemente eingebaut werden sollten und in einer kleinen Veranstaltung weniger. Aber Menschen an allen Orten sollten sich fragen, wie ein Sich-Sammeln in die Gnade und Barmherzigkeit Gottes hier angemessen stattfinden und dabei örtliche kulturelle Bräuche widerspiegeln kann.

8. Die Sendung kann verschiedene Handlungen einschliessen, aber sie sollte die Gemeinde in die Welt hinaus senden, um in Liebe zu dienen und Zeugnis für die Freiheit des Lebens in Christus, für die Gerechtigkeit, den Frieden und die Bewahrung der Schöpfung nach Gottes Willen abzulegen.

Die Sendung wird all das aufnehmen und in die Tat umsetzen, womit die Liturgie die Gemeinde zum Handeln aufgerufen hat. Sie kann durch ein Post-Communio-Gebet gekennzeichnet sein, das die Abendmahlsempfänger der Sendung Christi verpflichtet, durch Singen, einen Segen beim Weggehen, ein Wort der Entlassung, evtl. das Mitgeben der heiligen Kommunion an die Abwesenden, oder die Verteilung von Speisen an Bedürftige.

9. Die Teilhabe am verkündeten Wort und am Gebet der Gemeinde ist Teilhabe an Christus. Es ist auch Christus, der, in der Kraft des Heiligen Geistes, alle dazu einlädt, seine heilige Gabe zu essen und zu trinken.

Trotz allem sollten Gottesdienstteilnehmer, die nicht in der Lage sind, überhaupt das Abendmahl oder die eine oder andere der heiligen Gaben zu empfangen, nicht verletzt werden oder das Gefühl haben, nicht willkommen zu sein. Sie sollten ermutigt werden, so weit wie möglich teilzunehmen und Christus, der sich selbst für diese anderen seines Volkes hingibt, in Liebe und Anbetung zu erkennen sowie sich selbst als durch die Taufe zu Christus zugehörig zu verstehen und für den Tag der vollen Einheit unter den Christen zu beten.

10. Die umfassenden Möglichkeiten, die hier aufgelistet sind, sollten die einfache vorgeschlagene Ordnung nicht verdunkeln: diese Liturgie kann in grosser Einfachheit gefeiert werden oder als umfangreicher Versuch einer lokalen Gemeinschaft in Richtung auf ein Modell für die Zukunft.

Das Modell ist recht einfach (siehe *Ordo*, S. 43). Und mit einer klaren Wort- und Abendmahlsstruktur werden ökumenische Gruppen vor Ort dazu ermutigt, zu entdecken, wie diese grosse Gabe Gottes neu und glaubwürdig entfaltet werden kann. Weder sollte ein einfacher Gottesdienst jedoch die zentralen Elemente der Gabe Christi auslassen, noch sollte ein kunstvoll ausgestalteter oder experimenteller Gottesdienst sie verdecken.

11. Wenn eine Liturgie anhand dieser Vorschläge vorbereitet wird, werden Texte für die Hauptteile der Eucharistie am besten aus Gebeten ausgewählt, die eine weite ökumenische Anerkennung gefunden haben.

Bei der Auswahl der Texte für die Liturgie, einschliesslich der Bibelübersetzung, sollte sorgfältig auf die Verwendung inklusiver Sprache geachtet werden. Unterschiedliche Kulturen werden verschiedene Lösungen suchen, aber man sollte es sich zum Ziel setzen, immer die Sprache zu finden, die möglichst viele in die volle Teilnahme am Gebet einschliesst.

Gemäss den vorläufigen Richtlinien der ÖRK-Vollversammlung in Canberra[6] sollten biblische Sprache und bedeutende traditionelle Formeln beibehalten werden.

ANMERKUNGEN

[1] "Die Eucharistische Liturgie: liturgischer Ausdruck der Konvergenz erzielt in Taufe, Eucharistie und Amt", Verlag Otto Lembeck, Frankfurt/Main, 1983; Sonderdruck. "Die eucharistische Liturgie von Lima", Ökumenische Perspektiven von Taufe, Eucharistie und Amt, hg. von Max Thurian, Faith and Order Paper No.116, Verlag Otto Lembeck, Frankfurt/Main, 1983, Anhang, S.213-235. Die "Lima-Liturgie", ein nicht-offizieller Text der Kommission für Glauben und Kirchenverfassung, wurde verfasst, um in liturgischer Form die theologische Konvergenz zum Ausdruck zu bringen, die in dem offiziellen Text "Taufe, Eucharistie und Amt" erzielt wurde.

[2] *Taufe, Eucharistie und Amt*, Frankfurt/Main, 1982.

[3] S.9-17.

[4] "Eucharistie", Abschn.27.

[5] *Taufe, Eucharistie und Amt*, "Amt", Abschn.8.

[6] Vgl. Per Harling (Hg.), *Worshipping Ecumenically: Orders of Service from Global Meetings with Suggestions for Local Use*, Genf, WCC, 1995, S.3-4.

Das grundlegende Modell *(ordo)* des eucharistischen Gottesdienstes

SICH-SAMMELN der Gemeinde in die Gnade, die Liebe und Gemeinschaft des dreieinigen Gottes

WORTTEIL

> *Lesen* aus den Schriften des Alten und des Neuen Testaments
>
> *Verkündigen* des gekreuzigten und auferstandenen Jesus Christus als Grund unserer Hoffnung
>
> (unseren Glauben bekennen und singen)
>
> und von da aus für alle in Not sowie für die Einheit *Fürbitte tun*
>
> (den Friedensgruss austauschen, um unsere Gebete zu bestätigen und uns auf das Abendmahl vorzubereiten)

ABENDMAHLSTEIL

> über Brot und Kelch *Dank sagen*
>
> *Essen und Trinken* der heiligen Gaben der Gegenwart Christi
>
> (Sammeln für alle Notleidenden)
>
> und von da aus

IN DIE WELT AUSGESANDT WERDEN (Sendung)

Folgende Personen wirkten an der Ausarbeitung dieses Textes mit:

Pfr. Robert Gribben (uniert)
Pfr. Dr. Dennis Hughes (presbyt.)
Pfr. Brian Jemmot (angl.)
Pastor Gerd Kerl (uniert)
Prof. Dr. Gordon Lathrop (luth.)
Prof. Dr. Jaci Maraschin (angl.)
Frau Joan Matthews (bapt.)
Pfr. Rodney Matthews (bapt.)
Pfr. Dr. Thomas Best (Disciples of Christ)
Pfrin. Dr. Janet Crawford (angl.)
Pfrin. Dr. Dagmar Heller (uniert)

Darüber hinaus wurden unsere Diskussionen durch die Beiträge von P. Elias Thandikayil (oriental.-orth.) bereichert, der an der meisten unserer Sitzungen teilnahm.

Celebraciones de la Eucaristía en Contextos Ecuménicos

UNA PROPUESTA

Reunidos un grupo de cristianos de diferentes iglesias y confesiones de todo el mundo en el Instituto Ecuménico del Château de Bossey, Suiza, del 12 al 21 de mayo de 1995, examinaron el creciente fenómeno de las celebraciones de la eucaristía en contextos ecuménicos.

Los participantes en el encuentro dieron gracias a Dios por la amplia influencia de la Liturgia de Lima[1] en muchas iglesias y por los pasos provisionales que en algunas ocasiones han avanzado estas iglesias en el espíritu de la Liturgia de Lima y del documento *Bautismo, Eucaristía y Ministerio*.[2] También tomaron nota de que ha habido celebraciones de la eucaristía en encuentros ecuménicos internacionales, en actos ecuménicos regionales y locales y en pequeñas comunidades ecuménicas. Observaron que estas celebraciones, en el espíritu de la Liturgia de Lima, a menudo han ido más allá de la simple presentación de una tradición litúrgica, en sus formas históricas o actuales, a los cristianos congregados, muchos de ellos de otras tradiciones. Más bien lo que ha aparecido es el desafío de una nueva forma de oración ecuménica que surge del interés en facilitar la oración común a la comunidad concreta reunida, desde la convergencia teológica que va surgiendo de muchas fuentes, desde una exploración académica continuada y compartida de la herencia litúrgica de los cristianos y desde un afán por ver esa herencia celebrada en formas apropiadas a la dignidad y los dones de contextos culturales humanos específicos en todo el mundo.

Una parte importante de entre nosotros, liturgistas, teólogos y pastores, hemos examinado este fenómeno en más detalle. Bajo la disciplina del grupo más amplio y en constante debate con el mismo, nos hemos sentido movidos a proponer, bajo nuestra propia iniciativa y responsabilidad, el siguiente esquema y directrices para quienes se hallen involucrados en la planificación del culto eucarístico en un contexto ecuménico. En el planteamiento de esta propuesta nos han ayudado especialmente tres textos clásicos y significativos en relación a la eucaristía:

1. El relato, en Lucas 24:13-35, del Cristo resucitado que, por medio de su interpretación viva de las escrituras y su presencia en el partimiento del pan, transforma a dos discípulos desesperanzados y los envía en misión;
2. El relato del siglo segundo de Justino Mártir (1 Apología, 67) sobre la forma de la eucaristía antigua el domingo, incluyendo congregarse, leer las escrituras, predicar, interceder, sacar los alimentos, dar gracias, comer y beber, enviar a los ausentes y recoger para los pobres;

• Traducido del inglés por Rogelio Prieto.

3. La información de Ireneo de Lyón, hacia finales del siglo segundo, sobre la ocasión en que, como demostración de unidad, Aniceto, el obispo de Roma "cedió la acción de gracias" en la mesa eucarística de la iglesia romana a Policarpo, el obispo de Esmirna (Eusebio, Historia Eclesiástica, 5:24:11-18).

También nos han sido de gran ayuda dos extendidos y crecientes resultados del movimiento ecuménico: la convergencia *litúrgica* en un esquema común de la celebración eucarística, patente en la vida cultal de muchas iglesias, y la convergencia *teológica* en cuanto al significado y gracia de la eucaristía que representa la sección de la "Eucaristía" de BEM.[3]

Lo que sigue son sugerencias, ofrecidas en un espíritu de amor y oración, que presentamos a la consideración de quienes estén proyectando la celebración de una eucaristía en un contexto ecuménico. Ninguna de ellas tiene la intención de criticar las liturgias de las iglesias participantes o las tradiciones litúrgicas de denominaciones, confesiones o comuniones cristianas. Se presentan, más bien, como una propuesta sólida y descriptiva con el propósito de urgir a los organizadores a no olvidar el espíritu de la Liturgia de Lima: una celebración litúrgica reconocible por todos y que, no obstante, nos llama a ir más allá de nuestra propia experiencia, hacia una unidad más amplia.

En el esquema de culto eucarístico que aquí presentamos y en nuestras varias celebraciones siguiendo este modelo hemos encontrado un testimonio a la fe católica histórica. También hemos encontrado en ello una forma sencilla de celebración que se puede celebrar en una rica variedad de maneras, que responde a las necesidades del mundo en el momento actual y que es susceptible de inculturación en muchos lugares. Este modelo básico *(ordo)* se encuentra en la última página de este documento. Este esquema es consecuente con el listado dado en BEM,[4] pero nuestra presentación procura mostrar la simplicidad y claridad inherente del culto eucarístico, hacer patente su estructura subyacente, hacer evidente qué partes son esenciales (y cuáles opcionales) y sugerir tanto el movimiento como la continuidad del culto en su totalidad, así como las relaciones dinámicas entre sus partes.

También hemos encontrado que estos descubrimientos nos han llevado a importantes conclusiones en cuanto a la unidad cristiana. Por ejemplo: estamos muy conscientes de que a menudo son las cuestiones relacionadas con el ministerio y la autoridad las que mayormente impiden a los cristianos el acercarse juntos a la mesa del Señor. Estamos muy conscientes de lo complejas y sensibles que son estas áreas. Aún así, seguimos preguntándonos si las iglesias, sobre la base de la aceptación de este modelo por parte de todas las comuniones participantes, estarían dispuestas a ofrecerse mutuamente una "hospitalidad eucarística provisional" (es decir, invitar a todos los presentes en el acto ecuménico a recibir la comunión), al menos en encuentros ecuménicos importantes.

Ahora bien, cualquiera que sea la respuesta a esta cuestión, pediríamos a los grupos de cristianos involucrados en la planificación de cultos eucarísticos en un contexto ecuménico que se plantearan con nosotros las siguientes preguntas:

1. ¿Reconocen en este modelo litúrgico la fe católica histórica que une a su iglesia con las otras iglesias cristianas?

2. ¿Reconocen en este modelo litúrgico la presentación del mundo en que vivi-
mos, haciendo claramente manifiesta su condición y proclamando su transfor-
mación en Cristo?

3. Si es así, ¿cuáles son las implicaciones de estos reconocimientos?

A fin de ayudarles en su planificación y para fundamentar estas preguntas,
compartimos con ustedes las siguientes convicciones. Están pensadas para ser leí-
das junto con el esquema *(ordo)* para el culto eucarístico que se encuentra en la
página 50.

*1. La celebración de la eucaristía en un contexto ecuménico incluye una clara
liturgia de la palabra y una clara liturgia de la mesa.*

Este evento de palabra y mesa debería ser precedido por una santa convocación
de la asamblea en la gracia, amor y koinonía del Dios Trino y seguido por el
apropiado envío de la asamblea al testimonio y servicio. En relación a esta convocación y envío, ver los párrafos 7 y 8 a continuación.

*2. En una eucaristía así, la liturgia de la palabra incluye dos claros compo-
nentes:* lectura de las escrituras *del Antiguo y del Nuevo Testamento y* proclamación *de Jesucristo crucificado y resucitado como el origen y fundamento de
nuestra vida en la gracia de Dios. Las lecturas y la predicación deberían juntamente llevar a la asamblea a responder a la palabra con intercesión por las
necesidades del mundo y por la unidad de la iglesia, con confesión de la fe y con
canción.*

La confesión de la fe debería tener lugar o bien aquí, tras la homilía, o bien en
preparación para la liturgia de la mesa, usando el texto original del Credo Niceno
(Constantinopla, 381 d.C.) que es el que expresa la más amplia medida de con-
senso doctrinal entre las iglesias.

Una colecta recogida para los necesitados o para apoyar alguna causa acordada
de antemano también podría ser una respuesta apropiada en este momento, unida
a las intercesiones, o bien podría tener lugar al final de la liturgia de la mesa.

Los textos bíblicos deberían ser cuidadosamente escogidos en relación a la
ocasión y teniendo en cuenta los diversos leccionarios de las iglesias participantes.

La proclamación de Cristo tendrá lugar normalmente en forma de un sermón
preparado. En grupos más pequeños también podría tener lugar involucrando el
predicador a la asamblea en una reflexión activa sobre la palabra.

La liturgia de la palabra también podría incluir otros elementos que respondan
a y apoyen estos componentes, por ejemplo la meditación sobre la palabra en
silencio, el canto de himnos y de canciones contemporáneas, el canto de salmos,
el canto de himnos clásicos breves apropiados para la festividad del día *(kontakia)*
y de himnos o antífonas compuestas de versículos de salmos que pueden acom-
pañar la lectura de las escrituras *(prokeimena)*, así como otros tales elementos
litúrgicos de las tradiciones orientales, o versos de aleluya y secuencias y otros
tales elementos de la tradición occidental. El darse mutuamente la paz puede con-
cluir y sellar las intercesiones y servir como preparación para la liturgia de la
mesa.

3. En una eucaristía así, la liturgia de la mesa incluye dos claros componentes: una acción de gracias *en la mesa y el* comer y beber *comunitariamente el pan y la copa de la acción de gracias, los santos dones de la presencia viva y activa de Jesucristo. La acción de gracias y la comunión juntamente deben llevar entonces a la asamblea a la misión.*

La acción de gracias debería incluir el histórico diálogo *(sursum corda)*, la alabanza a Dios por la creación y la redención, las palabras de Cristo en la institución de la cena, el memorial explícito *(anamnesis)* de la pasión, muerte y resurrección de Jesucristo, la oración explícita por el advenimiento del día de Dios, expresado en invocación al Espíritu Santo *(epiclesis)* y conmemoraciones, el "amén" de toda la asamblea y el Padrenuestro. La mejor forma de proclamación de esta acción de gracias es con frecuentes respuestas de toda la asamblea.

El uso de un solo pan y de una sola copa grande debería ser considerado seriamente.

La colecta para los necesitados puede también tener lugar al final de la liturgia de la mesa, pero no debería ser omitida ni debería ser usada para gastos eclesiásticos ni para cubrir los gastos del evento. La colecta podría consistir en dones de comida para los hambrientos.

La liturgia de la mesa puede también incluir una presentación ceremonial de las ofrendas, una invitación a la comunión y el canto de canciones de comunión clásicas o modernas.

4. El evento completo de una eucaristía así debería ser musical, desplegándose la estructura general de la acción de la asamblea en la diversidad cultural de canción y movimiento de las iglesias del mundo.

La música, así como el espacio litúrgico con su arte visual, debería servir al discurrir esencial de la estructura del rito, no obscurecerlo. Debería involucrar a la asamblea en ese movimiento. Se ha de tener mucho cuidado, por ejemplo, al escoger las palabras de himnos y canciones que expresen lo más claramente posible la fe católica común, las lecturas bíblicas de la celebración, su lugar en el orden, el sentido del domingo o festividad y la unidad de la Iglesia.

La mutua participación de nuestras diversas herencias musicales, de nuestra creatividad, y la exploración de nuestras culturas han significado una contribución vital al culto ecuménico en los últimos años. Hemos aprendido que cada cultura tiene un rico don que aportar al culto, que el culto puede ser enriquecido con muchos estilos y ritmos musicales, escogidos cuidadosamente y con sensibilidad para su función litúrgica.

5. La celebración de una eucaristía así supone una asamblea que participa y muchos ministerios litúrgicos. Su unidad es mejor servida por la presidencia de una persona, a fin de servir a la unidad y continuidad de la totalidad de la liturgia y dar lugar a los dones presentes en la asamblea.

La celebración de la eucaristía en un contexto ecuménico debería, hasta donde sea posible, contar con la activa participación de toda la asamblea, a la vez que se respetan las disciplinas eclesiásticas. En la planificación deberían estar involucrados miembros, tanto ordenados como laicos, de todas las tradiciones representadas. También debería contar con el ministerio litúrgico de cristianos, tanto laicos como ordenados, en la lectura, el canto, la dirección del canto, oración, danza, servir y recoger.

Debería presidir un solo pastor, presbítero u obispo cuyo ministerio es reconocido por una de las iglesias participantes. "Para cumplir su misión, la Iglesia necesita personas que sean publica y continuamente responsables de señalar su fundamental dependencia de Jesucristo, proveyendo así, dentro de la multiplicidad de los dones, un foco de su unidad".[5] Se debería reflexionar cuidadosamente sobre este liderazgo. Quien preside puede pertenecer al liderazgo de una de las iglesias anfitrionas locales. Normalmente quien preside saludará a la asamblea, predicará, proclamará la acción de gracias y bendecirá a la asamblea al enviarles. La presidencia puede a veces ejercerse cediendo el lugar a otro predicador o a otra persona que dirija la plegaria eucarística. La "concelebración", entendida como presidencia por un grupo de ministros ordenados de diferentes confesiones, suscita más problemas ecuménicos que los que resuelve.

Los ministros, laicos y ordenados, que dirigen este culto pueden estar cada uno revestido de maneras que sean reconocibles como proclamación de nuestro común bautismo en Cristo y como representación de toda la asamblea. Otros signos de la festividad o del culto específico, tomados de las vestiduras cristianas históricas o de las culturas actuales de las iglesias pueden distinguir a los ministros principales, especialmente a quien preside.

6. En la planificación de una celebración eucarística así, se ha de considerar la posibilidad de tener la celebración en un domingo u otra festividad cristiana como señal del misterio de la resurrección que nos une.

En muchos lugares del mundo hay la necesidad de recuperar el sentido especial del domingo. La Cena del Señor pertenece en principio al Día del Señor. Aún más, el ecumenismo es central, no periférico, en la vida de las iglesias. Esto no pretende excluir la elección de otros días en aquellas situaciones en que un domingo o festividad no sean factibles para un acto ecuménico concreto.

7. La convocación puede incluir diversas acciones, pero debería siempre traer a la asamblea, que lleva en sí la necesidad y anhelos del mundo y la realidad de cada localidad, a la gracia y misericordia de Dios.

Tal convocación está basada en nuestro común bautismo en el misterio del Dios Trino y por tanto en la Iglesia. Esta convocación puede incluir el cantar las alabanzas de Dios, la confesión y perdón o alguna otra conmemoración bautismal, una llamada a la adoración o una salutación bíblica, un *kirie* o letanía de acceso, *Gloria in excelsis* u otra doxología y una oración colecta o introito tradicional. No se sugiere que todas estas formas de convocación deban ser usadas, ni que se planifiquen más posibles elementos para un gran evento o menos para uno pequeño, sino que las personas de cada lugar necesitan preguntarse cual es la forma apropiada *aquí* para convocar a la gracia y misericordia de Dios, reflejando las costumbres culturales locales.

8. La despedida puede incluir diversas acciones, pero debería siempre enviar a la asamblea a servir en amor y a dar testimonio de la libertad de la vida en Cristo y de la justicia, paz e integridad de la creación que Dios quiere.

La despedida ha de recoger y representar todas las maneras en que la liturgia ha movido a la asamblea a la acción. Puede estar marcada por una oración de poscomunión encomendando a los comulgantes a la misión de Cristo, por el canto, una bendición de despedida, una palabra de envío, el posible envío de la santa comunión o de otros dones a los que se encuentran ausentes, o el envío de comida a los pobres.

9. *La participación en la palabra proclamada y en las oraciones de la asamblea* es participación en Cristo. Es también Cristo quien, en el poder del Espíritu, invita a todos a comer y beber su santo don.

En todo caso, se debe evitar que los participantes en la liturgia que no puedan recibir la comunión en todo o en uno de los santos dones se sientan avergonzados o rechazados. Se les debería animar a participar hasta donde les sea posible, a contemplar en amor y adoración a Cristo que se da a sí mismo a aquellos otros de su pueblo, a verse a sí mismos como también pertenecientes a Cristo por el bautismo, y a orar por el día de una unidad cristiana más plena.

10. *La extensa lista de opciones aquí presentada no debería oscurecer la simplicidad del orden propuesto: esta liturgia podría celebrarse con gran simplicidad o con amplia experimentación local con vistas a que vaya surgiendo un modelo común para el futuro.*

El esquema es bastante sencillo (ver el *ordo* en la página 50) y, partiendo de la base de una estructura clara de palabra y mesa, se anima a los grupos ecuménicos locales a descubrir cómo este gran don de Dios puede ponerse de manifiesto de nuevo y fielmente. Un culto sencillo, por otra parte, no debería omitir los elementos centrales del don de Cristo, en tanto que uno elaborado o experimental no debería oscurecerlos.

11. *Al preparar una liturgia siguiendo estas propuestas, los textos para las partes principales de la eucaristía deberían ser escogidos de entre las oraciones que han tenido una amplia recepción ecuménica.*

En la selección de textos para la liturgia, incluyendo la elección de la versión de las escrituras que se usará, se debería prestar una cuidadosa atención al uso de lenguaje inclusivo. Las diferentes culturas requerirán diferentes soluciones, pero el objetivo es dar siempre con un lenguaje que incluya a todas las personas que sea posible en la oración. Siguiendo las directrices provisionales de la Asamblea de Canberra del Consejo Mundial de Iglesias,[6] el lenguaje bíblico y las fórmulas tradicionales importantes deberían ser preservadas.

NOTAS

[1] "The Eucharistic Liturgy: Liturgical Expression of Convergence in Faith Achieved in Baptism, Eucharist and Ministry", Ginebra, CMI, 1983; reimpresión de "The Eucharistic Liturgy of Lima", *Ecumenical Perspectives on Baptism, Eucharist and Ministry*, ed. Max Thurian, Faith and Order paper no. 116, Ginebra, CMI, 1983, Apéndice II, págs. 225-246. La "Liturgia de Lima", documento no oficial de la Comisión de Fe y Constitución, se elaboró para expresar en forma litúrgica las convergencias teológicas alcanzadas en el documento oficial *Bautismo, Eucaristía y Ministerio*.

[2] Faith and Order paper no. 111, Ginebra, CMI, 1982.
[3] Págs. 9-17.
[4] "Eucharist", pár. 27, págs. 15-16.
[5] BEM, "Ministry", pár. 8, pág. 21.
[6] Ver Per Harling, de., *Worshipping Ecumenically: Orders of Service from Global Meetings with Suggestions for Local Use*, Ginebra, CMI, 1995, págs. 3-4.

Esquema Fundamental *(Ordo)* del Culto Eucarístico

CONVOCACIÓN de la asamblea a la gracia, amor y koinonía del Dios Trino

LITURGIA DE LA PALABRA

Lectura de las escrituras del Antiguo y Nuevo Testamentos

Proclamación de Jesucristo crucificado y resucitado como fundamento de nuestra esperanza

(y confesión y canto de nuestra fe)

e *Intercesión* por todos los necesitados y por la unidad

(darse mutuamente la paz como sello de nuestras oraciones y preparación para la mesa)

LITURGIA DE LA MESA

Acción de gracias sobre el pan y la copa

Comer y beber los santos dones de la presencia de Cristo

(recoger colecta para los necesitados)

y

SER ENVIADOS (despedida) a la misión en el mundo

Las siguientes personas fueron miembros del grupo que elaboró este texto:

Rvdo. Robert Gribben (Igl. Unida)
Rvdo. Dennis Hughes (Presbiteriano)
P. Brian Jemmot (Anglicano)
Pastor Gerd Kerl (Igl. Unida)
Rvdo. Gordon Lathrop (Luterano)
Rvdo. Jaci Maraschin (Anglicano)
Sra. Joan Matthews (Bautista)
Rvdo. Rodney Matthews (Bautista)
Rvdo. Thomas Best (Discípulos de Cristo)
Rvda. Janet Crawford (Anglicana)
Rvda. Dagmar Heller (Igl. Unida)

Además, nuestro debate general fue enriquecido por el P. Elias Thandikayil (Ortodoxo Oriental), que pudo estar presente en muchas de nuestras sesiones.

The Lima Liturgy

1 Entrance psalm (with antiphon and *Gloria patri*; or hymn)

2 Greeting

P. The grace of our Lord Jesus Christ, the love of God, and the communion of the Holy Spirit be with you all.

C. *And also with you.*

3 Confession

C. Most merciful God,
>*we confess that we are in bondage to sin*
>*and cannot free ourselves.*
>*We have sinned against you*
>*in thought, word and deed,*
>*by what we have done*
>*and by what we have left undone.*
>*We have not loved you with our whole heart;*
>*we have not loved our neighbours as ourselves.*
>*For the sake of your Son, Jesus Christ, have mercy on us.*
>*Forgive us, renew us, and lead us,*
>*so that we may delight in your will*
>*and walk in your ways,*
>*to the glory of your holy name. Amen.*

4 Absolution

P. Almighty God
>gave Jesus Christ to die for us
>and for the sake of Christ forgives us all our sins.
>As a called and ordained minister of the church
>and by the authority of Jesus Christ,
>I therefore declare to you
>the entire forgiveness of your sins,
>in the name of the Father, and of the Son,
>and of the Holy Spirit.

C. *Amen.*

5 Kyrie litany

O. That we may be enabled to maintain the unity of the Spirit in the bond of peace and together confess that there is only one body and one Spirit, only one Lord, one faith, one baptism, let us pray to the Lord. [Eph. 4:3-5]

C. *Kyrie eleison*

O. That we may soon attain to visible communion in the body of Christ, by breaking the bread and blessing the cup around the same table, let us pray to the Lord. [1 Cor. 10:16-17]

C. *Kyrie eleison*

O. That, reconciled to God through Christ, we may be enabled to recognize each other's ministries and be united in the ministry of reconciliation, let us pray to the Lord. [2 Cor. 5:18-20]

C. *Kyrie eleison*

6 Gloria

Glory to God in the highest
– *And peace to God's people on earth.*

Lord God, heavenly King, almighty God and Father,
– *We worship you, we give you thanks.*

We praise you for your glory.
– *Lord Jesus Christ, only Son of the Father,*

Lord God, Lamb of God,
– *You take away the sin of the world: have mercy on us;*

You take away the sin of the world: receive our prayer;
– *You are seated at the right hand of the Father: have mercy on us.*

For you alone are the holy one,
– *You alone are the Lord,*

You alone are the Most High: Jesus Christ, with the Holy Spirit,
– *In the glory of God the Father,*

Amen.

LITURGY OF THE WORD

7 Collect

P. Let us pray:

Lord God, gracious and merciful, you anointed your beloved Son with the Holy Spirit at his baptism in the Jordan, and you consecrated him prophet, priest and king: pour out your Spirit on us again that we may be faithful to our baptismal calling, ardently desire the communion of Christ's body and blood, and serve the poor of your people and all who need our love, through Jesus

Christ, your Son, our Lord, who lives and reigns with you, in the unity of the Holy Spirit, ever one God, world without end.

C. Amen.

8 First lesson (Old Testament, Acts or Revelation)

9 Psalm of meditation

10 Epistle

11 Alleluia

12 Gospel

13 Homily

14 Silence

15 Nicene-Constantinopolitan Creed (text of 381)

We believe
in one God, the Father, the Almighty, maker of heaven and earth, of all that is, seen and unseen.

We believe
in one Lord, Jesus Christ, the only Son of God, eternally begotten of the Father, Light from Light, true God from true God, begotten, not made, of one Being with the Father; through him all things were made. For us and for our salvation he came down from heaven; by the power of the Holy Spirit he became incarnate from the Virgin Mary and was made man. For our sake he was crucified under Pontius Pilate; he suffered death and was buried; on the third day he rose again in accordance with the Scriptures; he ascended into heaven. He is seated at the right hand of the Father, he will come again in glory to judge the living and the dead, and his kingdom will have no end.

We believe
in the Holy Spirit, the Lord, the giver of life, who proceeds from the Father; with the Father and the Son he is worshipped and glorified; he has spoken through the prophets. We believe in one holy catholic and apostolic church. We acknowledge one baptism for the forgiveness of sins. We look for the resurrection of the dead, and the life of the world to come. Amen.

16 Intercession

O. In faith let us pray to God our Father, his Son Jesus Christ and the Holy Spirit.
C. Kyrie eleison
O. For the church of God throughout all the world, let us invoke the Spirit.

C. *Kyrie eleison*

O. For the leaders of the nations, that they may establish and defend justice and peace, let us pray for wisdom of God.

C. *Kyrie eleison*

O. For those who suffer oppression or violence, let us invoke the power of the Deliverer.

C. *Kyrie eleison*

O. That the churches may discover again their visible unity in the one baptism which incorporates them in Christ, let us pray for the love of Christ.

C. *Kyrie eleison*

O. That the churches may attain communion in the eucharist around one table, let us pray for the strength of Christ.

C. *Kyrie eleison*

O. That the churches may recognize each other's ministries in the service of their one Lord, let us pray for the peace of Christ.

C. *Kyrie eleison*

(spontaneous prayers of the congregation)

Into your hands, O Lord, we commend all for whom we pray, trusting in your mercy; through your Son, Jesus Christ, our Lord.

C. *Amen.*

LITURGY OF THE EUCHARIST

17 Preparation

O. Blessed are you, Lord God of the universe, you are the giver of this bread, fruit of the earth and of human labour, let it become the bread of life.

C. *Blessed be God, now and for ever!*

O. Blessed are you, Lord God of the universe, you are the giver of this wine, fruit of the vine and of human labour, let it become the wine of the eternal kingdom.

C. *Blessed be God, now and for ever!*

P. As the grain once scattered in the fields and the grapes once dispersed on the hillside and now reunited on this table in bread and wine, so, Lord, may your whole church soon be gathered together from the corners of the earth into your kingdom.

C. *Maranatha! Come Lord Jesus!*

18 Dialogue

P. The Lord be with you

C. *And also with you.*

P. Lift up your hearts.

C. *We lift them to the Lord.*

P. Let us give thanks to the Lord our God.

C. *It is right to give God thanks and praise.*

19 Preface

P. Truly it is right and good to glorify you, at all times and in all places, to offer you our thanksgiving, O Lord, Holy Father, Almighty and Everlasting God. Through your living Word you created all things, and pronounced them good. You made human beings in your own image, to share your life and reflect your glory.

When the time had fully come, you gave Christ to us as the Way, the Truth and the Life. He accepted baptism and consecration as your servant to announce the good news to the poor.

At the last supper Christ bequeathed to us the eucharist, that we should celebrate the memorial of the cross and resurrection, and receive his presence as food. To all the redeemed Christ gave the royal priesthood and, in loving his brothers and sisters, chooses those who share in the ministry, that they may feed the church with your word and enable it to live by your sacraments.

Wherefore, Lord, with the angels and all the saints, we proclaim and sing your glory:

20 Sanctus

C. *Holy, Holy, Holy...*

21 Epiclesis I

P. O God, Lord of the universe, you are holy and your glory is beyond measure. Upon your eucharist send the life-giving Spirit, who spoke by Moses and the prophets, who overshadowed the Virgin Mary with grace, who descended upon Jesus in the river Jordan and upon the apostles on the day of Pentecost.
May the outpouring of this Spirit of Fire transfigure this thanksgiving meal that this bread and wine may become for us the body and blood of Christ.

C. *Veni Creator Spiritus!*

22 Institution

May this Creator Spirit accomplish the words of your beloved Son, who, in the night in which he was betrayed, took bread, and when he had given thanks to you, broke it and gave it to his disciples, saying:

Take, eat: this is my body, which is given for you. Do this for the remembrance of me.

After supper he took the cup and when he had given thanks, he gave it to them and said:

Drink this, all of you: this is my blood of the new covenant, which is shed for you and for many for the forgiveness of sins. Do this for the remembrance of me. Great is the mystery of faith.

C. *Your death, Lord Jesus, we proclaim! Your resurrection we celebrate! Your coming in glory we await!*

23 Anamnesis

P. Wherefore, Lord, we celebrate today the memorial of our redemption: we recall the birth and life of your Son among us, his baptism by John, his last meal with the apostles, his death and descent to the abode of the dead; we proclaim Christ's resurrection and ascension in glory, where as our Great High Priest he ever intercedes for all people; and we look for his coming at the last.

United in Christ's priesthood, we present to you this memorial: Remember the sacrifice of your Son and grant to people everywhere the benefits of Christ's redemptive work.

C. *Maranatha, the Lord comes!*

24 Epiclesis II

P. Behold, Lord, this eucharist which you yourself gave to the church, and graciously receive it as you accept the offering of your Son whereby we are reinstated in your covenant. As we partake of Christ's body and blood, fill us with the Holy Spirit that we may be one single body and one single spirit in Christ, a living sacrifice to the praise of your glory.

C. *Veni Creator Spiritus!*

25 Commemorations

O. Remember, Lord,

your one, holy, catholic and apostolic church, redeemed by the blood of Christ. Reveal its unity, guard its faith, and preserve it in peace.

Remember, Lord, all the servants of your church: bishops, presbyters, deacons, and all to whom you have given special gifts of ministry.

(Remember especially....)

Remember also all our sisters and brothers who have died in the peace of Christ, and those whose faith is known to you alone: guide them to the joyful feast prepared for all peoples in your presence, with the blessed Virgin Mary, with the patriarchs and prophets, the apostles and martyrs... and all the saints for whom your friendship was life.

With all these we sing your praise and await the happiness of your, kingdom where with the whole creation, finally delivered from sin and death, we shall be enabled to glorify you through Christ our Lord.

C. *Maranatha, the Lord comes!*

26 Conclusion

P. Through Christ, with Christ, in Christ, all honour and glory is yours, Almighty God and Father, in the unity of the Holy Spirit, now and for ever.

C. *Amen.*

27 The Lord's prayer

O. United by one baptism
   in the same Holy Spirit and the same body of Christ, we pray as God's sons
   and daughters:
C. *Our Father,...*

28 The peace

O. Lord Jesus Christ,
   you told your apostles: Peace I leave with you, my peace I give to you.
   Look not on our sins but on the faith of your church; in order that your will
   be done, grant us always this peace and guide us towards the perfect unity
   of your kingdom for ever.
C. *Amen.*
P. The peace of the Lord be with you always
C. *And also with you.*
O. Let us give one another a sign of reconciliation and peace.

29 The breaking of the bread

P. The bread which we break is the communion of the body of Christ, the cup of
   blessing for which we give thanks is the communion in the blood of Christ.

30 Lamb of God

C. *Lamb of God, you take away the sins of the world,*
   have mercy on us.
   Lamb of God, you take away the sins of the world,
   have mercy on us.
   Lamb of God, you take away the sins of the world
   grant us peace.

31 Communion

32 Thanksgiving prayer

P. In peace let us pray to the Lord
   O Lord our God, we give you thanks for uniting us by baptism in the body
   of Christ and for filling us with joy in the eucharist. Lead us towards the
   full visible unity of your church and help us to treasure all the signs of reconciliation you have granted us. Now that we have tasted of the banquet
   you have prepared for us in the world to come, may we all one day share
   together the inheritance of the saints in the life of your heavenly city,
   through Jesus Christ, your Son, our Lord, who lives and reigns with you in
   the unity of the Holy Spirit, ever one God, world without end.
C. *Amen.*

33 Final hymn

34 Word of mission

35 Blessing

P. The Lord bless you and keep you.
   The Lord make his face shine on you and be gracious to you.
   The Lord look upon you with favour and give you peace.
   Almighty God, Father, Son and Holy Spirit, bless you now and forever.
C. *Amen.*

III

Eucharistic Services:
Worship Texts from, and
Inspired by, the Consultation

Africa

Gathering/Greeting/Singing/Peace

Jesus, we are here for you. Jesus sieh, hier sind wir, wir sind für dich da. Jésus nous sommes là prêts à te servir. Jesus estamos preparados para ti.

Call to worship

Leader	We have come together
All	*with our longing,*
	with our faith and our doubts.

Leader	We have come together
All	*seeking the depths of faith*
	in prayer and praise.

Leader	We have come together
All	*to share, to learn, to grow*
	in unity and in the love of God.

Leader	Let us be silent before the face of God.

Silence

Music

Confession

Leader	We belong together,
All	*like members in one body.*

Leader	When there is dissension within the body,
All	*Lord have mercy on us.*

Song

Patrick Matsikenyiri: Zimbabwe

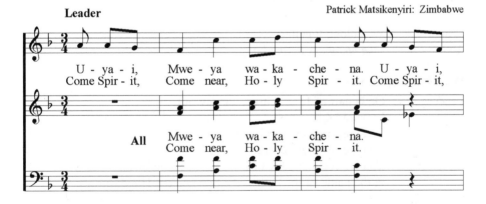

U - ya - i ne - ta - ri - ro.
Come, with a hope a - bid - ing.

U - ya - i ne - ta - ri - ro.
Come, with a hope a - bid - ing.

Leader	If one member suffers,
All	*all suffer together with it.*
Leader	When we lack compassion,
All	*Lord, have mercy on us.*

Uyai

Leader	If one member is honoured,
All	*all rejoice together with it.*
Leader	When we lack thankfulness and shared joy,
All	*Lord, have mercy on us.*

Uyai

Leader	We belong together,
All	*Like members in one body.*

Words of forgiveness

Leader	On behalf of Jesus Christ, our saviour,
	I assure you:
	You are forgiven, forgive others.
	You are restored, restore others.
	You are reconciled with God, be reconciled with others,
	in the name of the Father, the Son and the Holy Spirit.
All	*Amen.*

Song of praise

Mungaka, Cameroon

Ba ni ngye - ti Ba Ya - we, ba ni ngye - ti Ba Ya - we,
Let us praise the Lord our God, let us praise the Lord our God,
Prei - sen laßt uns Gott, den Herrn, prei - sen laßt uns Gott, den Herrn,
Ren - dons grâ - ce au Sei - gneur, ren - dons grâ - ce au Sei - gneur,
A - la - be - mos al Se - ñor, a - la - be - mos al Se - ñor,

ba ni ngye - ti Ba Ya - we, A - men. Hal - le - lujah,
let us praise the Lord our God. A - men. Hal - le - lujah.
prei - sen laßt uns Gott, den Herrn, A - men. Hal - le - lu - ja.
ren - dons grâ - ce au Sei - gneur, A - men. Al - lé - lu - ia,
a - la - be - mos al Se - ñor, A - mén. A - le - lu - ya,

Hal - le - lu - jah, Hal - le - lu - jah, A - men.
Hal - le - lu - jah. Hal - le - lu - jah. A - men.
Hal - le - lu - ja. Hal - le - lu - ja. A - men.
Al - lé - lu - ia, Al - lé - lu - ia, A - men.
A - le - lu - ya, A - le - lu - ya, A - mén.

Prayer (collect)

Sung response

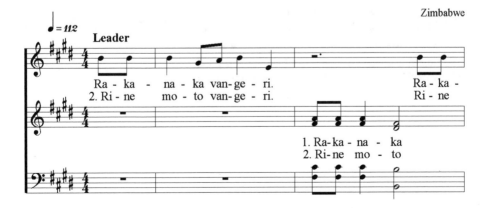

Zimbabwe

♩ = 112   Leader

Ra - ka - na - ka van - ge - ri. Ra - ka -
2. Ri - ne mo - to van - ge - ri. Ri - ne

1. Ra - ka - na - ka
2. Ri - ne mo - to

The Gospel is good. Over and over I tell you it is good.
The Gospel has power. Over and over I tell you it has power.

Scripture readings:

Old Testament: Jer. 29:10-14

Sung response: *Rakanaka*

Gospel: John 6:41-51

Sung response: *Rakanaka*

Reflection

Silence

Intercession (with sung response)

Uyai

Song

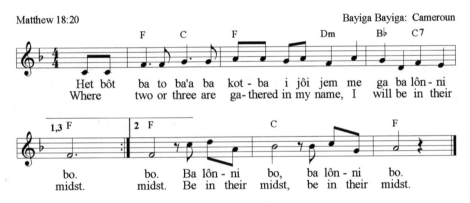

Matthew 18:20 · Bayiga Bayiga: Cameroun

Het bôt ba to ba'a ba kot - ba i jôi jem me ga ba lôn - ni bo.
Where two or three are ga-thered in my name, I will be in their midst.

Ba lôn - ni bo, ba lôn - ni bo.
Be in their midst, be in their midst.

Leader	The Lord be with you.
All	*And also with you.*
Leader	Lift up your hearts.
All	*We lift them to the Lord.*
Leader	Let us give thanks to the Lord our God.
All	*It is right to give him thanks and praise.*
Leader	It is indeed right,

from east to west, from north to south,
in all the seasons of our life,
to give thanks to you, O God, O Living One.
Dwelling beyond time and space, you abide among us,
embracing the world with your justice and love.
And so, with all baptized of every race and land,
with the multitudes in heaven
and the countless choirs of angels,
we praise your glorious name
and join their unending hymn:

Song

Patrick Matsikenyiri: Zimbabwe

Eucharistic prayer

Leader   Holy God, holy and mighty one, holy immortal:
                you we praise and glorify,
                you we worship and adore.
                You formed the earth from chaos;
                you encircled the globe with air;
                you created fire for warmth and light;
                you nourished the lands with water.

                You moulded us in your image,
                and with mercy higher than the mountains,
                with grace deeper than the seas,
                you blessed the Israelites
                and cherished them as your own.

That also we, estranged and dying,
might be adopted to live in your Spirit,
you called us through the life and death of Jesus,
who in the night in which he was betrayed,
took bread, and gave thanks;
broke it, and gave it to his disciples,
saying: Take and eat; this is my body, given for you.
Do this for the remembrance of me.

Again, after supper, he took the cup,
gave thanks and gave it for all to drink,
saying: This cup is the new covenant in my blood,
shed for you and for all people
for the forgiveness of sin.
Do this for the remembrance of me.

Together as the body of Christ
we proclaim the mystery of his death:

All   *Christ has died, Christ is risen, Christ will come again.*

Leader   With this bread and cup we remember your Son,
the first-born of your new creation.
We remember his life for others,
and his death and resurrection,
which renews the face of the earth.
We await his coming
when, with the world made perfect through your wisdom,
all his sons and sorrows will be no more.

All   *Amen. Come, Lord Jesus.*

Leader   Holy God, holy and merciful one,
holy and compassionate,
send upon us and this meal your Holy Spirit,
whose breath revives us for life,
whose fire rouses us to love.
Enfold in your arms all who share this holy food.
Nurture in us the fruits of the Spirit,
that we may be a living tree,
sharing your bounty with all the world.

All   *Amen. Come, Holy Spirit.*

Leader   Holy and benevolent God,
receive our praise and petitions,
as Jesus received the cry of the needy,
and fill us with your blessing,
until, needy no longer and bound to you in love,
we feast forever in the triumph of the Lamb:
through whom all glory and honour is yours,
O God, O Living One, with the Holy Spirit,
in your holy church, now and forever.

All

S.C. Molefe: Xhosa, South Africa

From the Lumko Song Book © Lumko Institute, P.O. Box 5058, 1403 Delmenville, Republic of South Africa. Transcription and English, Dave Dargie © Lumko Institute.

The Lord's prayer

Leader   In the community of the Spirit we pray:
All   *Our Father (each in his or her own language)*

The breaking of the bread

Leader   The bread which we break
            is the communion of the body of Christ,
            the cup of the blessing for which we give thanks
            is the communion in the blood of Christ.

Lamb of God (Iropa)

Patrick Matsikenyiri: Zimbabwe

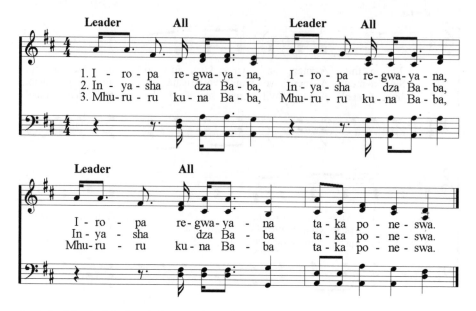

1. I - ro - pa re - gwa - ya - na,   I - ro - pa re - gwa - ya - na,
2. In - ya - sha dza Ba - ba,   In - ya - sha dza Ba - ba,
3. Mhu - ru - ru ku - na Ba - ba,   Mhu - ru - ru ku - na Ba - ba,

I - ro - pa re - gwa - ya - na ta - ka po - ne - swa.
In - ya - sha dza Ba - ba ta - ka po - ne - swa.
Mhu - ru - ru ku - na Ba - ba ta - ka po - ne - swa.

1. It's the blood of the Lamb that saved us all.
2. It is the grace of our God that saved us all.
3. Yululate to the Father who saved us all.

Communion

Thanksgiving prayer

Leader   We have received bread and wine,
the body and the blood of your Son, Jesus Christ.

All   *We thank you, Lord*

Leader   We have shared your living Word
in reflection and prayer, in faith and hope.

All   *We bless you, Lord*

Leader   We have been joyfully singing your glory
with body, mind and spirit before your face.

All   *We praise you, Lord. Amen.*

Song *Masithi, Amen*

Blessing

Latin America

Introito

Momento musical
Saludo

C. La gracia de nuestro Señor Jesucristo, el amor de Dios y la comunión del Espíritu Santo estén con todos.

Confesión

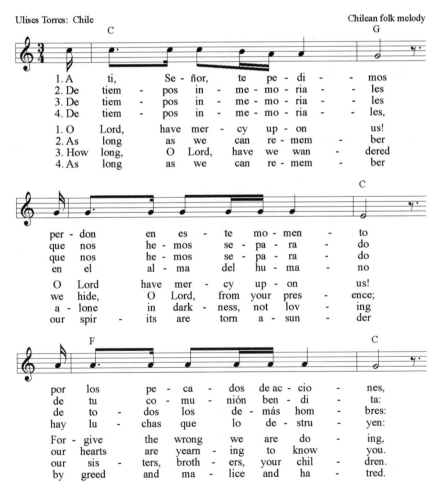

Ulises Torres: Chile

Chilean folk melody

1. A ti, Se - ñor, te pe - di - - mos
2. De tiem - pos in - me - mo - ria - - les
3. De tiem - pos in - me - mo - ria - - les
4. De tiem - pos in - me - mo - ria - - les,

1. O Lord, have mer - cy up - on us!
2. As long as we can re - mem - ber
3. How long, O Lord, have we wan - dered
4. As long as we can re - mem - ber

per - don en es - te mo - men - to
que nos he - mos se - pa - ra - do
que nos he - mos se - pa - ra - do
en el al - ma del hu - ma - no

O Lord have mer - cy up - on us!
we hide, O Lord, from your pres - ence;
a - lone in dark - ness, not lov - ing
our spir - its are torn a - sun - der

por los pe - ca - dos de ac - cio - nes,
de tu co - mu - nión ben - di - ta:
de to - dos los de - más hom - bres:
hay lu - chas que lo de - stru - yen:

For - give the wrong we are do - ing,
our hearts are yearn - ing to know you.
our sis - ters, broth - ers, your chil - dren.
by greed and ma - lice and ha - tred.

pa	la	bras	y		pen	sa	mien	tos.
per	do	na	nues	tro	pe	ca		do.
per	do	na	nues	tro	pe	ca		do.
per	do	na	nues	tro	pe	ca		do.
our	words	and	thoughts	that	of	fend		you.
O	Lord,	have	mer	cy	up	on		us.
O	Lord,	have	mer	cy	up	on		us.
O	Lord,	have	mer	cy	up	on		us.

Español © Ulises Torres. English © Alvin Schutmaat.

T. Amen.

Kyrie eleison

Gloria

T.

Glo-ria a Dios, Glo-ria a Dios, Glo-ria en los cie-los!
Glo-ry to God, Glo-ry to God, Glo-ry in the highest!

A Dios la glo-ria por siem-pre! Al-le-lu-ya, A-men!
To God be glo-ry for-e-ver!

Al-le-lu-ya, A-men! Al-le-lu-ya, A-men!

2. Gloria a Dios, Gloria a Dios,
   Gloria a Jesucristo. . .

2. Glory to God, Glory to God,
   Glory to Christ Jesus. . .

3. Gloria a Dios, Gloria a Dios,
   Gloria sea al Espíritu. . .

3. Glory to God, Glory to God,
   Glory to the Spirit. .

LITURGIA DE LA PALABRA

Colecta del Quinto Domingo de Pascua

C. Dios omnipotente, conocerte es la vida eterna: Otórganos la perfección del conocimiento de tu Hijo Jesucristo, para que él sea el camino, la verdad, y la vida; que sigamos firmes sus huellas en el camino que conduce a la vida eterna; por Jesucristo, tu Hijo, nuestro Señor, que vive y reina contigo en la unidad del Espíritu Santo, un solo Dios, por siempre jamás.

T. *Amen.*

Lectura de la Epístola: 2 Tesalonicenses 2: 13-17

Salmo 67 (in English)

C. May God be gracious to us and bless us/ and make his face to shine upon us.

T. *May God be gracious to us and bless us/ and make his face to shine upon us.*

R. That your way may be known upon earth,/your saving power among all nations.

L. Let the peoples praise you, O God;/let all the peoples praise you.

R. *Let the nations be glad and sing for joy,/for you judge the peoples with equity and guide the nations upon earth.*

L. Let the peoples praise you, O God/let all the peoples praise you.

R. *The earth has yielded its increase;/God, our God, has blessed us.*

L. May God continue to bless us:/let all the ends of the earth revere him.

C. *May God be gracious to us and bless us/ and make his face to shine upon us.*

T. May God be gracious to us and bless us/ and make his face to shine upon us.

Lectura del Evangelio: Mateo 7: 15-29 (Antes de la lectura todos dicen: ¡Gloria a ti, Cristo Señor! Depués de la lectura: ¡Te alabamos, Cristo Señor!)

Homilia

Silencio

Credo (in English)

C. We believe that God is Father, that he cares with special affection for the suffering, the little ones, the migrants, the poor, the exploited.

W. *I believe, Lord, but come and increase my faith.*

C. We believe that Jesus came "to announce the good news to the poor, to give sight to the blind and to set free those who are ill-treated".

M. *I believe, Lord, but come and increase my faith.*

C. We believe that the Holy Spirit reveals his love to little ones and gives us strength to struggle side by side with our comrades to form a fraternal world in accordance with the will of the Father.

T. *I believe, Lord, but come and increase my faith. Amen.*

Intercesiones (sentados) (Intercessions will be offered by several participants in their own languages. After each intercession we will sing: "Oh! Come, wondrous rumour, wind noisy and impetuous, renew all our life: it is resurrection!")

Zeni Lima: Brazil   Jaci Maraschin: Brazil

Vem for - te ru - í - do, ven - to im - pe - tu - o - so

e a vi - da re - no - va: é res - sur - rei - ção.

Oh! Come, wondrous rumour, wind noisy and impetuous, renew all our life: it is
resurrection!

Potuguese Zeni Lima, Music and English translation, Jaci Maraschin © Rua Leão XIII, 230 ap 11, Rudge Ramos,
São Bernardo do Campo 09735-220, São Paulo - SP, Brazil.

LITURGIA DE LA EUCARISTIA

Ofrenda y presentación de los dones

Preparación del altar

Himno

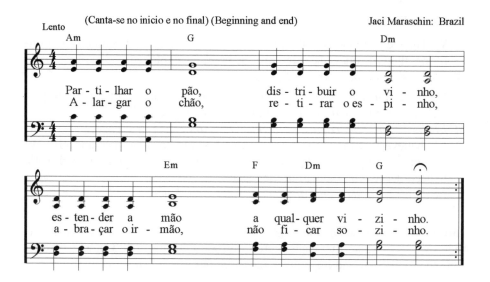

Lento   (Canta-se no inicio e no final) (Beginning and end)   Jaci Maraschin: Brazil

Am   G   Dm

Par - ti - lhar o   pão,   dis - tri - buir o   vi - nho,
A - lar - gar o   chão,   re - ti - rar o es - pi - nho,

Em   F   Dm   G

es - ten - der a   mão   a qual - quer vi - zi - nho.
a - bra - çar o ir - mão,   não fi - car so - zi - nho.

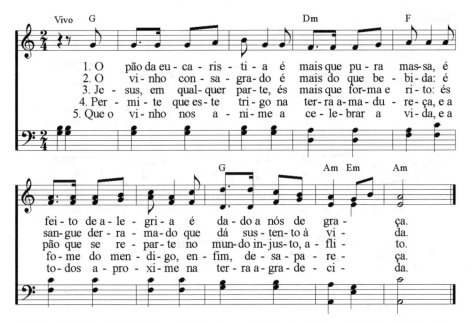

1. O   pão da eu - ca - ris - ti - a   é   mais que pu - ra   mas-sa, é
2. O   vi - nho   con - sa - gra - do é   mais do que be - bi - da: é
3. Je - sus, em   qual-quer par-te, és   mais que for-ma e   ri - to: és
4. Per - mi - te   que es - te   tri - go na   ter - ra a-ma-du - re - ça, e a
5. Que o   vi - nho nos   a - ni - me a   ce - le - brar a   vi - da, e a

fei - to de a - le - gri - a   é   da - do a nós de   gra - ça.
san-gue der - ra - ma-do que   dá sus - ten-to à   vi - da.
pão que se   re - par-te no   mun-do in-jus-to, a - fli - to.
fo - me do men - di - go, en - fim, de - sa - pa - re - ça.
to - dos a - pro - xi - me na   ter - ra a-gra - de - ci - da.

Jaci Maraschin © Rua Leão XIII, 230 ap 11, Rudge Ramos, São Bernardo do Campo 09735-220, São Paulo - SP, Brazil.

Preparación:

C. Bendito seas, Señor, Dios del universo, por este pan, fruto de la tierra y del tra-
bajo del hombre, que recibimos de tu generosidad y ahora te presentamos: él
será para nosotros pan de vida.

T. *Bendito seas por siempre, Señor.*

C. Bendito seas, Señor, Dios del universo, por este vino, fruto de la vida y del tra-
bajo del hombre, que recibimos de tu generosidad y ahora te presentamos: él
será para nosotros bebida de salvación.

T. *Bendito seas, por siempre, Señor.*

C. Así como las espigas, que estaban dispersas por las colinas, se han reunido
sobre esta mesa en el pan y en el vino, asi también, Señor, sea reunida muy
pronto toda tu Iglesia de los confines de la tierra en tu Reino.

Sursum Corda

Himno

Panama

¡A - rri - ba   los co - ra - zo - nes! Va - ya - mos to -
We   lift   up   our hearts to you,   God. The bread of life

dos al pan de vi - da,   que es, fuen - te de glo - ria e - ter -
we pre - sent to - geth - er,   the   source of e - ter - nal glo -

na, de for - ta - le - za y de a - le - grí - a.   1. A
                                                    2. Per -
ry, the taste of joy   for your hun - gry peo - ple. 1. We
                                                      2. For -

ti a - cu - di - mos se - dien - tos ¡Ven Se - ñor!
do - na nues - tros pe - ca - dos ¡Ven Se - ñor!
come to you,   tired and thirs - ty, come O Lord.
give us all   our of - fen - ses, come O Lord,

Te - ne - mos fe en tu mis - te - rio ¡Ven Se - ñor!
Por e - so en ti con - fi - a - mos ¡Ven Se - ñor!
We trust your gift in this mys - tery, come O Lord.
for you are a - ble to free us, come O Lord.

Que - re - mos dar - te la vi - da ¡Ven Se - ñor!
Y ha - lla - re - mos las fuer - zas ¡Ven Se - ñor!
We of - fer you all our liv - ing, come O Lord,
Re - new our hope with your par - don, come O Lord,

Con sus do - lo - res y di - chas ¡Ven Se - ñor!
Pa - ra ol - vi - dar las o - fen - sas ¡Ven Se - ñor!
with all its sor - row and search - ing, come O Lord.
till we for - give those who wrong us, come O Lord.

English Terry MacArthur © 1997 World Council of Churches, Geneva.

C. El Señor esté con vosotros.

T. Y con tu espíritu.

C. Levantad vuestros corazones.

T. Los levantamos al Señor.

C. Demos gracias al Señor, nuestro Dios.

T. Es justo y necesario dar gracias y alabar a Dios.

Prefacio

C. En verdad, es justo y necesario darte gloria y ofrecerte nuestra acción de gracias, siempre y en todo lugar, a ti, Padre santo, Dios todopoderoso y eterno. Por
tu Palabra viva, creaste todas la cosas y las hiciste buenas; formaste al ser
humano a tu imagen para que participara de tu vida y reflejara tu gloria. Al lle-
gar a la plenitud de los tiempos nos diste a Cristo como el Camino, la Verdad
y la Vida. El aceptó el bautismo y la consagración como tu Siervo para anun-
ciar las buenas nuevas a los pobres. Te damos gracias porque por el Espíritu
Santo, nos has guiado a toda verdad, y nos has dado poder para proclamar tu
Evangelio a las naciones y servirte como sacerdotes. Por eso, Señor, con los
ángeles y todos los santos, proclamamos tu gloria cantando:

Sanctus

Misa Popular Salvadoreña: El Salvador

Muy movido

San - to, San - to, San - to, San - to, San - to, San - to es nues - tro
Ho - ly, Ho - ly, Ho - ly, Ho - ly, Ho - ly, Ho - ly is our
Hei - lig, Hei - lig, Hei - lig, Hei - lig, Hei - lig, Hei - lig, un - ser
Très saint, Très saint, Très saint, Très saint, Très saint, Très saint, no - tre

Dios, Se - ñor de to - da la tie - rra, San - to, San - to es nues - tro
God, God the Lord of earth and hea - ven, Ho - ly Ho - ly is our
Gott, Gott des Him - mels und der Er - de. Hei - lig, Hei - lig, un - ser
Dieu Sei - gneur de tou - te la ter - re, Très saint, Très saint, no - tre

Dios, San - to, San - to, San - to, San - to, San - to, San - to es nues - tro
God. Ho - ly, Ho - ly, Ho - ly, Ho - ly, Ho - ly, Ho - ly is our
Gott. Hei - lig, Hei - lig, Hei - lig, Hei - lig, Hei - lig, Hei - lig, un - ser
Dieu. Très saint, Très saint, Très saint, Très saint, Très saint, Très saint, no - tre

C7

Dios, Se - ñor de to - da la his - to - ria San - to San - to es nues-tro
God, God the Lord of all of his - tory, Ho - ly, Ho - ly is our
Gott,Gott, der Herr uns 'rer Ge-schich-te, Hei - lig, Hei - lig, un - ser
Dieu Sei-gneur de tou - te l'his-toi - re, Très saint, Très saint, no - tre

Fine

F   F   Bb   C

Dios. Que a-com - pa - ña a nues-tro pue-blo, que vi - ve en nues-tras
God. Who ac-com - pa - nies our peo-ple, who lives with - in our
Gott. Er ist mit uns heut' und mor-gen, er lebt in un - serm
Dieu. Qui ac-com - pa - gne son peu-ple char - gé de tous les

F   C   F

lu - chas, del u - ni - ver - so en-te-ro el ú - ni-co Se - ñor.
strug - gles, of all the earth and hea-ven the one and on - ly Lord.
Rin - gen, auf Er - den wie im Welt-all ist er al-lein der Herr.
far - deaux, u - ni - que Sei-gneur de la ter - re, de l'u - ni - vers.

Bb   C

Ben - di - tos los que en su nom - bre el E - van - ge - lio a-
Bless - ed those who in the Lord's name an - nounce the ho - ly
Lo - bet die in sei - nem Na - men das E - van - ge - lium
Bé - nis soient ceux qui an - non - cent l'E - van - gi - le

F   C7   **D.C. al Fine**

nun-cian, la bue-na y gran no - ti - cia de la li - be - ra - ción.
Gos-pel, pro - claim-ing forth the GoodNews: our li - be - ra - tion comes.
kün-den, die gu - te fro - he Bot-schaft: Be - freiung ist uns nah.
de la bon - ne nou - vel - le de no - tre li - bé - ra - tion.

Introducción y Final

Bb   F   C7   F   Bb   F

Bb   C   F

Español and Music, El Salvador. English, © Linda McCrae. Deutsch, Dieter Trautwein © Strube Verlag,
München.

Institución

C. Santo eres, Señor Dios del universo y tu gloria es sin medida. Estamos agrade-cidos porque Cristo nos legó la Eucaristía para que celebráramos el memorial de la cruz y la resurrección, y recibiéramos su presencia como alimento. Que este espíritu creador de cumplimiento a las palabras de tu hijo amado, el cual, la noche en que iba a ser entregado, tomó el pan, lo bendijo en la acción de gra-cias, lo partió y lo dió a sus discípulos diciendo: Tomad y comed todos de él, porque esto es mi cuerpo, que será entregado por vosotros. Haced esto en memoria de mi. Del mismo modo, acabada la cena, tomó el cáliz, lo bendijo en la acción de gracias, y lo pasó a sus discípulos diciendo: Tomad y bebed todos de él porque esta cáliz es la Nueva Alianza en mi sangre, que será der-ramada por vosotros y por muchos para el perdón de los pecados. Haced esto en memoria de mi.

T. *Cristo ha muerto, Cristo ha resucitado. Cristo volverá.*

Anamnesis

C. Bondadoso Dios, celebramos hoy el memorial de nuestra redención: evocamos el nacimiento y la vida de tu Hijo entre nosotros, su bautismo por Juan, su última cena con los Apóstoles, su muerte y su descenso a la morada de los muertos, proclamamos su resurrección y ascensión a los cielos, donde lleva a cabo su ministerio de Sumo Sacerdote intercediendo por todos nosotros: esper-amos su retorno glorioso.

T. *¡Maranatha. Ven Señor!*

Epiclesis

C. He aquí, Señor, esta Eucaristía que tu mismo diste a tu Iglesia y, que miseri-cordiosamente recibes, así como aceptas la ofrenda de tu Hijo por la que volve-mos a participar en tu Pacto. Envia sobre esta Eucaristía tu Espíritu dador de vida.

Que al verter este Espíritu de fuego se transfigure esta comida de acción de gracias: y que este pan y este vino sean para nosotros el Cuerpo y la Sangre de Cristo. Y al participar del Cuerpo y la Sangre de Cristo, llénanos de tu Espíritu Santo, para que seamos un cuerpo y un espíritu en Cristo, une ofrenda viva par la alabanza de tu gloria.

T.

Jacques Berthier: Taizé, France

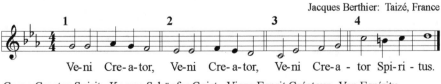

Ve-ni Cre-a-tor, Ve-ni Cre-a-tor, Ve-ni Cre-a - tor Spi-ri - tus.

Come Creator Spirit. Komm Schöpfer Geist. Viens Esprit Créateur. Ven Espíritu Creador.

Conmemoraciones

C. Recuerda, Dios de amor, a tu única Iglesia, santa, católica y apostólica, redimida por la sangre de Cristo. Revela su unidad, guarda su fe y presérvala en paz. Acuérdate de todos los siervos de tu Iglesia: obispos, presbiteros, diáconos, y de todos aquellos a quienes tú has dado ministerios especiales.

Recuerda también a nuestras hermanas y nuestros hermanos que han muerto en la paz de Cristo, y a aquellos cuya fe sólo tu conoces; llévalos hacia la fiesta de la alegría preparada para todos los pueblos en tu presencia, con la bienaventurada Virgen María, con los patriarcas y los profetas, los apóstoles y los mártires... y todos los santos que vivieron en tu amistad. Con ellos cantamos tu alabanza y esperamos la felicidad de tu Reino, donde podremos, con toda la creación, libres ya del pecado y de la muerte, glorificarte por Cristo, nuestro Señor.

Conclusión

C. Por él, con él y en él, a ti, Dios padre omnipotente, en la unidad del Espíritu Santo, todo honor y toda gloria por los siglos de los siglos.

T. *Amén.*

El Padrenuestro

C. Unidos por el único bautismo, en el mismo Espíritu en el mismo Cuerpo de Cristo, podemos decir con confianza la oración de los hijos y las hijas de Dios:

T. *Padre nuestro (each in his or her own language)*

La Paz

C. Señor Jesucristo, que dijiste a los apóstoles: Mi paz os dejo, mi paz os doy, no mires nuestros pecados sino la fe de tu Iglesia, y conforme a tu palabra, concédele siempre la paz y llévala hacia la unidad perfecta de tu Reino, por los siglos de los siglos. Amén.

La paz del Señor sea con vosotros.

T. *Y con tu Espíritu.*

C. Démonos un signo de reconciliación y de paz.

Simei Monteiro: Brazil

El partimiento del pan

C. El pan que partimos es la comunión en el Cuerpo de Cristo, la copa de bendición por la que damos gracias es la comunión en la sangre de Cristo.

Comunión

Oración de Acción de Gracias

C. Oremos en paz al Señor: Oh Señor nuestro Dios, te damos gracias por unirnos mediante el bautismo en el Cuerpo de Cristo, y por colmarnos de gozo en la Eucaristía. Guianos hacia la plena unidad visible de tu Iglesia y ayúdanos a atesorar todas las señales de reconciliación que nos has brindado. Ahora que hemos saboreado una anticipación del festín de tu Reino, haz que participemos todos juntos de la herencia de los santos en luz, por Jesucristo, tu Hijo, Señor nuestro, que vive y reina contigo, en la unidad del Espíritu Santo, un solo Dios, por los siglos de los siglos.

T. *Amén.*

Bendición

C. El Espíritu de Verdad os conduzca a toda la verdad, os conceda la gracia de confesar que Jesucristo es el Señor y de proclamar la palabra y las obras de Dios, y que la bendición de Dios todopoderoso, Padre, Hijo y Espíritu Santo sea con vosotros ahora y siempre.

T. *Amén.*

Envío

C. Recibiréis poder, cuando haya venido sobre vosotros el Espíritu Santo, y me seréis testigos.

T. *Gracias sean dadas a Dios.*

Himno de clausura

Can-te-mos a nues-tro Dios,   El es el Dios de la
God is up-lift-ing the peo-ple!   God is the pow-er with-

vi - da,   por - que El es - tá con no -
in us!   Hope is our mus - ic and

so - tros crean - do la es-pe - ran - za y la li - ber - tad.
free-dom our song and to - geth-er our voic-es will ring.

Music, Edwin Mora and Español, Ester Camac © G., SBL, Apdo 901-1000 San José, Costa Rica. English © Bret Hesla.

The Service of the Grains

(people gather outside the chapel in a circle on the grass)

L. Great things indeed the Lord did for us,
and we rejoiced.
Those who sow in tears
will reap with songs of joy.
They went out, went out weeping,
carrying the seed.
They come back, come back singing,
bringing in the sheaves.

Song
(During the singing of this song, grains of wheat will be distributed to each one
with the words, "the grace of God be with you". We respond "and also with you".
The grains are to be held during the first part of the worship.)

Jaci Maraschin: Brazil

1. Quando o Se - nhor nos li - ber - tar do ca - ti -
1. When God, our Lord, will lead us out of de - so -
2. When God, our Lord, comes gra - cious - ly to us ap -
3. When God, our Lord, will be for us the sole de -
4. When God, our Lord, will re - u - nite us on that

vei - ro pa - re - ce - rá um so - nho,
la - tion, it's going to seem we're dream - ing.
pear - ing, it's going to seem we're dream - ing.
light, it's going to seem we're dream - ing.
day, it's going to seem we're dream - ing.

a nos - sa bo - ca vai sor - rir con -
Then will our mouths be filled with ex - al -
Then, joy - ful - ly, we'll see the King - dom
Our won - dering eyes will con - tem - plate this
Then, all our tears will have been wiped a -

Cm   Ab 7+   G   Cm

ten - te	e can - ta - re - mos	sem pa -	rar.
ta - tion;	in joy for ev - er	we will	sing.
near - ing	and this full - fil - ment	makes us	free.
light,	the col - or of a	bright new	world.
way;	heav - en and earth will	then be	one.

2. Quando o Senhor nos restaurar, enfim, a aurora parecerá um sonho. As nossas mãos vão se encontrar, felizes, e a liberdade vão firmar.

3. Quando o Senhor se constituir nosso horizonte parecerá um sonho. Os nossos olhos hão de ver, surpresos, um novo mundo a germinar.

4. Quando o Senhor nos reunir, vitorioso, parecerá um sonho. As nossas lágrimas terão passado e a terra e o céu se encontrarão.

Jaci Maraschin © 1988 Rua Leão XIII, 230 ap 11, Rudge Ramos, São Bernardo do Campo 09735-220, São Paulo - SP, Brazil English, Sonya Ingwersen © 1989 WCC.

Short meditation on the grain

Gloria (during the singing the group enters the chapel)

Luke 2:14   Pablo Sosa: Argentina

Cueca ♩. = 72

F   C7

Glo - ria, glo - ria,	glo - ria	en las al - tu - ras a	Dios.
Eh - re, Eh - re,	Eh - re,	Eh - re im Him - mel sei	Gott.
Gloi - re, Gloi - re,	Gloi - re,	dans les lieux très - hauts à	Dieu.

C   F   C

Y en la tie - rra	paz pa - ra a - que - llos	que a - ma el Se - ñor.
Und auf Er - den	Fried' un - ter de - nen,	die ihn lie - ben.
Sur la ter - re	paix à ceux qui ai - ment	le Sei - gneur.

© Pablo Sosa, Camacuá 252, 1406 Buenos Aires, Argentina. German, Wolfgang Leyk. French, Joëlle Gouël © 1990 WCC.

LITURGY OF THE WORD

L. Let us pray:
  Loving God,
  You gave us this beautiful day
  and you gather us here in this chapel.
  You gave us your son as the living bread.
  We thank you.
  Help us to recognize your grace
  and to realize our brokenness.
  Let us find the unity
  of which your son spoke
  when he said, "May they all be one."

Song on the theme of the word of God

Old Testament reading: Lamentations 2:11-13

My eyes are worn out with weeping,
      my inmost being is in ferment,
my heart plummets
      at the destruction of my young people,
as the children and babies grow faint
      in the streets of the city.
They keep saying to their mothers,
      "Where is some food?"
as they faint like people wounded
      in the streets of the city,
as they breathe their last
      on their mothers' breasts.
To what can I compare or liken you,
      daughter of Jerusalem?
Who can rescue or comfort you,
      young daughter of Zion?
For huge as the sea is your ruin:
      who can heal you?

Hallelujah

Böhmische Brüder, 1544: Germany

Hal - le - lu - ja, Hal - le - lu - ja, Hal - le - lu - ja,

Hal - le - lu - ja. Ge - lobt sei Chri-stus, Ma - ri - en Sohn!

Gospel: Matthew 15:21-28

Meditation

Meditative music

The congregation is asked to reflect on our lamentations and our brokenness, and to begin to gather ideas to be brought together in the intercessions.

Affirmation of faith (to be said responsively)

Left   Jesus Christ is the image of the invisible God
              the firstborn of all creation,
              in him all things in heaven and on earth were created,
              all things, visible and invisible.

Right   *All things have been created through him and for him.*
              He himself is before all things,
              and in him all things hold together.

Left   He is the head of the body, the church;
              he is the beginning;
              the firstborn of the dead,
              so that he might come to have first place in everything.

Right   *For in him, the fullness of God was pleased to dwell,*
              and through him God was pleased to recognize all things,
              whether on earth or in heaven,
              by making place through the blood of his cross. (Col. 1:15-20)

Intercessions

L. I ask your prayers for peace in the life of the world
   (people are invited to pray for peace aloud in their own language or in silence)

   After each group of petitions we sing:

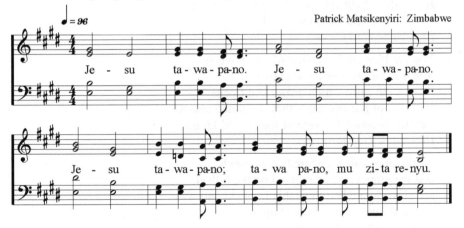

Patrick Matsikenyiri: Zimbabwe

Je - su ta - wa - pa-no. Je - su ta - wa - pa-no.

Je - su ta - wa - pa-no; ta - wa pa-no, mu zi-ta re-nyu.

Jesus, we are here for you. Jesus sieh, hier sind wir, wir sind für dich da. Jésus nous sommes là prêts à te servir. Jesus estamos preparados para ti.

L. I ask your prayers for the church around the world
Jesu tawa...

L. I ask your prayers for the broken in mind, body and spirit.

L. I ask your prayers for each one here.

L   May God who is full of tenderness and compassion hear these and the prayers of all who call on him.

L. We share one spirit and one body because we all share the one bread.

Let us therefore exchange a sign of peace with one another, and offer one another the grain we hold as a sign of our longing for unity.

The peace is exchanged.

L. Jesus said, Unless a grain of wheat falls into the earth and dies, it remains only a single grain; but if it dies it yields a rich harvest. [John 12:24]

Let us present our offerings of bread and wine and grain, and with them ourselves.

The bread and wine are brought in and afterwards the people bring their grain to the basket placed on the table.

LITURGY OF THE EUCHARIST

Preparation

L. You are blessed, Lord God of the universe.
You are the giver of this grain,
fruit of the earth which grows and ripens.
By work of human hands it is made into bread.
Let this become the bread of life.
C. *Blessed be God for ever.*

L. You are blessed, Lord God of the universe.
You are the giver of these grapes,
fruit of the earth which grows and ripens.
By work of human hands they are made into wine.
Let this become the wine of the eternal kingdom.
C. *Blessed be God for ever.*

L. As the grain once scattered in the fields
and the grapes once dispersed on the hillside
are now reunited on this table in bread and wine,
so, Lord, may your whole church
soon be gathered together
from the corners of the earth
into your kingdom.
C. *Maranatha. The Lord comes.*

Dialogue

L. The Lord be with you
C. And also with you.

L. Lift up your hearts.
C. We lift them to the Lord.

L. Let us give thanks to the Lord our God.
C. It is right to give God thanks and praise.

Preface

L. Yes, indeed, it is good to give you glory
   and to thank you, O God.
   You guide and nurture all human beings.
   You created all things and pronounced them good.
   You made us in your image
   to share your life and to mirror your glory.
   You gave Christ to us
   to be our friend and brother and to lead us into life.
   He makes you known to us.
   He unites us, the scattered ones, around his table.
   So we praise you with all your people
   and sing your glory:

Sanctus (sung as a canon)

Jacques Berthier: Taizé France

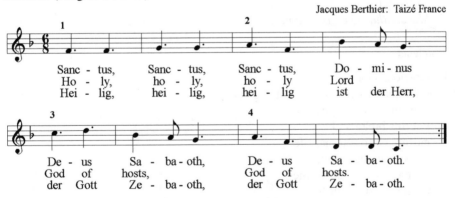

Sanc - tus, Sanc - tus, Sanc - tus, Do - mi - nus
Ho - ly, ho - ly, ho - ly Lord
Hei - lig, hei - lig, hei - lig ist der Herr,

De - us Sa - ba - oth, De - us Sa - ba - oth.
God of hosts, God of hosts.
der Gott Ze - ba - oth, der Gott Ze - ba - oth.

Music J. Berthier © Ateliers et Presses de Taizé, 71250 Taizé Communauté, France.

Institution

L. Remember what you have received from our Lord Jesus Christ,
   how on the night before he met with death,
   he came to table with those he loved.
   He took bread
   and praised you, God of all creation.
   He broke the bread among his disciples and said:

"Take this, all of you, and eat it.
This is my body given for you."

When supper was ended,
he took the cup of wine
and gave thanks to you, God of all creation.
He passed the cup among his disciples and said:
"Take this, all of you, and drink from it.
This is the cup of the new covenant sealed in my blood
for the forgiveness of sin.
Do this in remembrance of me."
This is the mystery of our faith.

C. *Christ has died*
Christ has risen
Christ will come again.

Anamnesis

L. With this bread and this wine we remember your Son
the firstborn of your new creation.
We remember his life lived for others,
and his death and resurrection
which renews the face of the earth.
We wait for him to come
to make whole what is broken and scattered
and to turn our tears into joy.

C. *Maranatha. The Lord comes.*

Epiclesis

L. Gracious God,
send upon us and these earthly gifts
your life-giving spirit.
Let this bread and wine
nurture us for eternal life.
As we eat and drink,
so may we be transformed
to show forth your love
and be united with our brothers and our sisters
still scattered around the world.

Commemorations

L. Remember, O Lord, your church throughout the world.
May we grow in unity, faith and love.
Remember all our sisters and brothers
whose broken lives were touched by your love
and who looked for wholeness in you:

– Mary Magdalene who brought the news of your resurrection;
– Peter whom you called to feed your sheep;
(people are invited to name others whose lives show God's love in action)

Remember all those today who live in brokenness and long for healing:
– the voiceless ones who through their pain and hope give you glory;
(a moment for naming others)

In solidarity with all these,
may we sing your praise
and await the happiness of your kingdom
where, with all your creation,
finally made whole and free,
we shall truly glorify you
through Christ our Lord.

C. *Maranatha. The Lord comes.*

Conclusion

L. Through Christ, with Christ, in Christ,
all honour and glory is yours,
Almighty God and Father,
in the unity of the Holy Spirit,
now and for ever.

C. *Amen.*

L. United by the one who is the bread of life we pray together:
Our father... (each in his or her own language)

L. The gifts of God for the people of God.

Lamb of God

Patrick Matsikenyiri: Zimbabwe

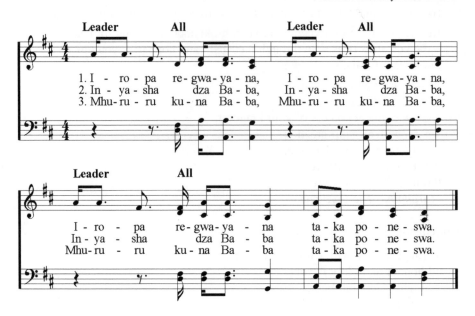

1. I - ro - pa re-gwa-ya - na, I - ro-pa re-gwa-ya - na,
2. In - ya - sha dza Ba - ba, In - ya-sha dza Ba - ba,
3. Mhu-ru - ru ku - na Ba - ba, Mhu-ru-ru ku-na Ba - ba,

I - ro - pa re-gwa-ya - na ta - ka po - ne-swa.
In-ya - sha dza Ba - ba ta - ka po - ne-swa.
Mhu-ru - ru ku-na Ba - ba ta - ka po - ne-swa.

1. It's the blood of the Lamb that saved us all.
2. It is the grace of our God that saved us all.
3. Yululate to the Father who saved us all.

Communion

(During the sharing of bread and wine we sing the following)

Per Harling: Sweden

1. För   li - vets   skull   ska   san - ning - en   bli
1. For the sake of   life   the   face   of   truth   will
1. Face   à   la   vie,   la   vé - ri - té   é -
1. Por   es - ta   vi - da   la   ver - dad   a -

syn - lig.   För   li - vets   skull   ska läng-tans frön slå
bright - en.   For the sake of   life   the seeds of hope will
cla - te,   face   à   la   vie   que gran-dis - se l'es-
lum - bra   por   es - ta   vi - da   va - le   es - pe-

	Dm	D7	Gm			
rot.	För	li - vets	skull	ska	fre - dens väg	bli
root.	For the sake	of	life	the	way of peace	will
poir,	face	à la	vie	que	la paix se	ré -
rar	por	es - ta	vi -	da	la paz tiene	un

F	F♯ dim		Gm	A7		Dm
tyd - lig	för dem som	vå - gar gå	för	li - vets	skull.
light - en	for those who	dare to walk–	for the sake	of	life.
pan - de	sur le che -	min ru - gueux -	face	à la	vie.
rum - bo	lo he - mos de -	ca - mi - nar,	pa - ra	vi -	vir.

2. För livets skull ger ännu marken gröda.
För livets skull bär jorden ännu kraft.
För livets skull ska alla få sin föda
ur denna jord vi fått - för livets skull.

3. För livets skull vänds vanmakten till vrede.
För livets skull ska rätten flöda fram.
För livets skull ska källor utav glädje
ge modet hopp och kraft - för livets skull.

4. För livets skull blev Gud ett barn, vår like.
För livets skull gav han sitt liv för oss.
För livets skull ska rättens rätta rike
bli synligt genom oss - för livets skull.

2. Face à la vie, répandons la semence,
face à la vie, que grandisse le grain,
face à la vie, que nul ne désespère
que tous aient part au pain–face à la vie.

3. Face à la vie, la justice se révolte,
face à la vie, élevons notre voix,
face à la vie, redonnons espérance
aux victimes du mal – face à la vie.

4. Face à la vie, c'est Dieu qui se révèle,
face à la vie, il a donné son Fils
face à la vie, il a ouvert son règne,
son Royaume est tout près – face à la vie.

****

2. For the sake of life the fields are being seeded.
For the sake of life there's still growth in the earth.
For the sake of life we'll share with all that need it
the bread from common soil - for the sake of life.

3. For the sake of life a righteous wrath needs power.
For the sake of life let streams of justice roll.
For the sake of life the springs of joy will mother
the newborn child of hope - for the sake of life.

4. For the sake of life our God became an infant.
For the sake of life he lived and died for all.
For the sake of life the time of God is constant.
The kingdom is at hand - for the sake of life.

****

2. Por esta vida está sembrado el campo
por esta vida hay crecimiento aún
por esta vida el pan de nuestra tierra
compartiremos hoy, para vivir.

3. Por esta vida se rebela el débil
por esta vida justicia fluirá
por esta vida cada primavera
renueva y da valor para vivir.

4. Por esta vida Dios se hizo pequeño
por esta vida el vivió y murió
por esta vida el verdadero Reino
en nuestra acción verán, para vivir.

Thanksgiving

A reading from Isaiah 65:17-25

Song

(During the singing of this song, we process out to stand in a circle on
the grass)

John M. C. Crum   French Carol

1. Now   the   green blade   ris - es   from   the   bur - ied
2. In   the   grave they   laid their Love whom   hate had
3. Christ came   forth   at   Eas - ter, like   the   ris - en
4. When   our   hearths are   win - try, griev - ing, or   in

grain;   wheat   that   in   dark   earth for
slain,   think - ing   that   their   Love   would
grain,   Je - sus, who   for   three days
pain,   Christ's warm touch can   call   us

man - y   days has   lain;   Love lives a - gain,   that
nev - er wake a - gain,   laid in   the   earth like
in   the grave had lain,   quick from the   dead the
back to   life a - gain,   fields of our   hearts that

with   the   dead   has   been:
grain that   sleeps un -   seen:
ris - en   One   is   seen:
dead   and   bare   have   been:

Love is come a - gain like wheat that ris - es green.

Song on the theme of growth or unity

(As we sing this song we give each other a sign of blessing)

Words of mission

(As we say these words, the grain will be scattered)

L. We now sow the grain
as a sign of God's shalom.

Let us go now in the peace and love of God,
to do his work and share his word.

C. *In the name of Christ. Amen.*

An Ecumenical Experiential Eucharist

An Account of the Closing Worship

RODNEY MATTHEWS

The climax

The work undertaken at the Lima liturgy workshop at the Ecumenical Institute, Bossey, in May 1995, culminated in a eucharist, the last of six such celebrations. This proved to be the living-out of what had been discovered during the ten days and is related in this volume. Thus there is good reason to describe this act of worship in some detail – both as a demonstration of how principles may be put into practice and as an example of the process that may be followed by others who try to work out the practical implications of the principles here described.

Before relating the detail of this final act of worship, however, it is necessary to refer to its background, including the other services which were shared. This is not a comprehensive report of all that was done in the workshop but an essential outline of what led up to, and contributed to, the final worship.

Cultural expression

In the first half of our time together three eucharists had been shared with the intention of drawing the participants into a variety of cultural expressions: these were from Latin America, Asia and Africa. They had been planned beforehand, as a way to experience something of the development of the Lima liturgy over the years in a variety of places and circumstances. Each involved some preliminary rehearsal of songs (and language) and actions. The setting of the room was different for each, and afterwards there was an opportunity to reflect and comment on the service and to learn from each other. In other acts of worship – morning and evening prayers – and at other informal times we enjoyed further expressions of the variety of our cultures and local experiences.

The study of liturgical principles and their application

In the context of receiving several addresses and cultural and contextual stories and in addition to participating in plenary discussions we also divided into four groups: one to produce a further definite statement in the light of the Ditchingham consultation; one to work on the practical implications of this in simplified form for small local ecumenical gatherings and to collate worship material; and two groups to prepare for further eucharistic celebrations in which we would all join as we progressed. Contact was maintained throughout between the four groups. Only as we moved towards the last two days did we establish a further group – drawn from the continuing four groups – this one to be responsible for arranging the final eucharist in a way that would test what we had ourselves discovered together in the process of our worship.

A eucharistic liturgy "without paper"

The result was moving, liberating but, perhaps above all not so much a unifying of rich diversity as a discovery of how this diversity is already at one in Christ.

No papers or books whatsoever were needed, except the copies of the scriptures to be read. Neither was it necessary to have a hymn rehearsal, since we used only those simple but profound Christian songs that had become familiar to us. We were therefore free from one of the main encumbrances to using our bodies in worship.

The gathering

We entered the chapel with seating "in the round", at the centre of which was the table. On this were flowers from the garden and, on a white linen cloth, a large loaf on a plate, an earthenware chalice and a jug of wine. We sat, in silent reflection on what had brought us here, until all were assembled.

A German poet recited by heart – in German, then in English – the simple poem he had composed only a day or two before as an expression of what had happened to his heart:

Kastanienblüten	Chestnut blossoms
Kalter Tag im Mai	Cold a day in May
in der Kapelle	and in the chapel
Singen, Schweigen, Beten	singing, silence, praying

Then, led by a Zimbabwean with his hand-held percussion instrument, we sang spontaneously over and over again, "Where two or three are gathered in my name I will be there in their midst." As we did so four members came, from the four corners of the earth, with two white robes and liturgical stoles to dress those whom we had decided beforehand should preside and assist – an American Lutheran presbyter and a Methodist laywoman from Malaysia. They were to wear, for all of us, the garments that represented our common baptism into Christ.

The president greeted us and we responded. He led us into an awareness of the presence of God who is "always more ready to hear than we to pray", forgiving us those things of which our conscience was afraid and about to give again things for which we scarcely dare ask. The scene was thus set for the liturgy of the word and the table. We were in no doubt as to why we had gathered.

The word

What scriptures are appropriate for such an occasion? Aware of the danger in "suiting ourselves" we allowed ourselves to be held within the context of the unity and continuity of the church. This was the Sunday before Ascensiontide and we opted, arbitrarily, for one of the many ecumenical lectionaries available, thus being at one on this day with Christians of many traditions who "sat" under the same text. Deuteronomy 34 was read in English by our lay leader from Malaysia, and we sang "alleluia" in response. Then, all standing, we listened to the president read John 16:12-24, a passage lending itself easily to being read in three languages – English, German and Spanish.

We sat as our organist improvised in modern but Bach-like style, evoking the mood of these lections, and afterwards remained for a moment in silence.

Then the president, remaining seated within the circle, proclaimed the word, speaking of the vision that held together in unity Moses and Jesus, and of the hope that is in us as Christ's people as we look forward to what is both promised and fulfilled in Christ.

He pleaded for help from the assembly to make up what he might lack in proclaiming such truth and, between moments of silent meditation, several members spoke simply and movingly as the Spirit led them, calling up our joyful expectation.

It was during this period that the president spoke for us all when he bid "bon voyage" to a sister bound for the Caribbean and having to depart before the end of the service – the most natural of warm touches that took nothing away from the dignity of worship but spoke volumes of the koinonia we had experienced.

As a Syrian Orthodox priest from India then recited for us the Nicene Creed in his own tongue we were united, in a language that none of us understood, in a truth to which we wholeheartedly gave our assent with an "amen".

Intercessory biddings were introduced, permitting both spontaneous petitions and choral kyries. We exchanged the sign of the peace which had broken down the wall of hostility and made us one. The word received, we were ready for the feast.

The table

To the rhythm of Cuban drums we sang "Arriba los corazones!" (we lift up our hearts!) as our attention focused on the table: the verses were sung in Spanish and all joined in the chorus we had picked up during our time together – *Ven Señor* (Come, O Lord!)

The great eucharistic prayer, with its dialogue, preface, sung sanctus, epiclesis, institution, anamnesis and commemoration, was led by the president. We sang throughout *ex corda*. We sang affirming "amens" to each phrase, until we reached the end with a rising crescendo of a triple "amen". As the Lord's prayer was recited in a single bold German voice, we all joined in quietly in the many tongues and versions of this single text, demonstrating our rich diversity.

The president and assistant served us with bread and wine as we moved from our places towards the central table, whilst quietly in the background brothers and sisters sang a Zimbabwean version of the "Agnus Dei" composed and led by one of the participants – *"Iropa regwyana taka po ne swa"* ("It's the blood of the Lamb that saved us all").

The sending

After a post-communion prayer a collection was taken for the street children of Brazil and handed over to our fellow-worker who was unable to speak her thanks as she received the token of our Christian solidarity. We were dismissed, sensing that the Lord would indeed bless us and keep us, and make his face to shine upon us and be gracious to us, and that he would lift up his countenance upon us and give us peace, and we left the chapel praising the name of God in a South African song, "Masithi: Amen". Outside on the grass in the morning sunshine, looking across the lake to the distant mountains, we broke into spontaneous applause – that means by which people today express approval that they cannot put into words. The supper was ended, the mission called.

Eine Messe für unsere Zeit

KURT ROSE UND WOLFGANG TEICHMANN

I. ANKOMMEN UND AUFRICHTEN

1 Eingangsmusik

Kurt Rose

Wolfgang Teichmann: Germany

2 Einladung

(Gerufen von drei Stimmen)
(three voices - A,B, and C - calling out)
1. Durchgang mit Fermaten und hineingesprochenen Texten.
1. First time through with fermata's and voices.

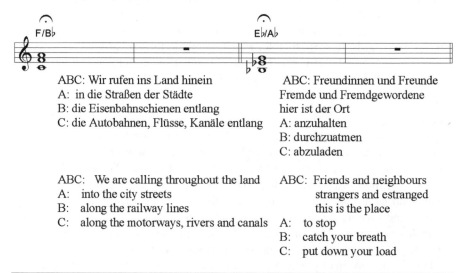

ABC: Wir rufen ins Land hinein
A: in die Straßen der Städte
B: die Eisenbahnschienen entlang
C: die Autobahnen, Flüsse, Kanäle entlang

ABC: Freundinnen und Freunde
Fremde und Fremdgewordene
hier ist der Ort
A: anzuhalten
B: durchzuatmen
C: abzuladen

ABC: We are calling throughout the land
A: into the city streets
B: along the railway lines
C: along the motorways, rivers and canals

ABC: Friends and neighbours
      strangers and estranged
      this is the place
A: to stop
B: catch your breath
C: put down your load

Text Kurt Rose; Musik Wolfgang Teichmann

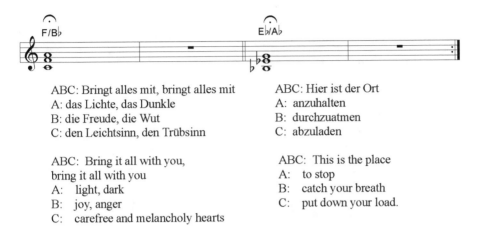

ABC: Bringt alles mit, bringt alles mit
A: das Lichte, das Dunkle
B: die Freude, die Wut
C: den Leichtsinn, den Trübsinn

ABC: Hier ist der Ort
A: anzuhalten
B: durchzuatmen
C: abzuladen

ABC: Bring it all with you,
bring it all with you
A: light, dark
B: joy, anger
C: carefree and melancholy hearts

ABC: This is the place
A: to stop
B: catch your breath
C: put down your load.

2. Durchgang ohne Fermaten, mit Improvisation, dann Überleitung und Lied Nr. 4 (Ort, wo das Leben entspringt)
2. Second time through improvised with no fermatas.

3   Kurzes Musikstück (es stellt das Chorlied 4 vor)

4   "Ort, wo das Leben entspringt"

Kurt Rose

Wolfgang Teichmann: Germany

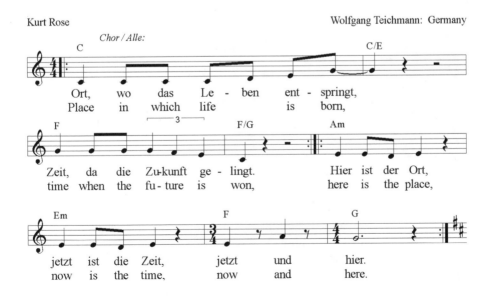

Ort,   wo   das   Le - ben   ent - springt,
Place   in   which   life   is   born,

Zeit,   da   die   Zu-kunft   ge - lingt.
time   when   the   fu - ture   is   won,

Hier   ist   der   Ort,
here   is   the   place,

jetzt   ist   die   Zeit,   jetzt   und   hier.
now   is   the   time,   now   and   here.

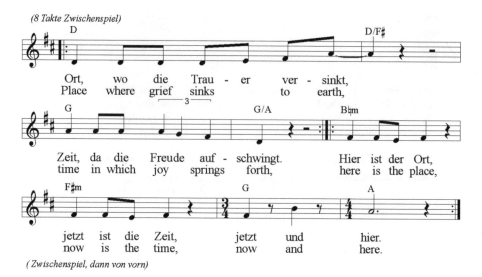

(8 Takte Zwischenspiel)

Ort, wo die Trau - er ver - sinkt,
Place where grief sinks to earth,

Zeit, da die Freude auf - schwingt. Hier ist der Ort,
time in which joy springs forth, here is the place,

jetzt ist die Zeit, jetzt und hier.
now is the time, now and here.

(Zwischenspiel, dann von vorn)

5 Unsere Situation

Liturg   Wir wenden uns Gott zu, Gott der innewohnenden
              und umgreifenden Kraft der Welt

              Öffne unsere Augen, Gott
              dass wir uns sehen, wie wir sind
              du folgst den Wegen der Menschen
              auch wenn wir hinauffliegen in den Himmel
              du bist zugegen
              auch wenn wir uns in Nacht verbergen
              Gib uns den Mut, Gott, uns zu sehen, wie wir sind

Chor und Gemeinde

Kurt Rose   Wolfgang Teichmann: Germany

Chor:

Du bist Hei - lung, du bist Rat.
You are heal - ing, you are wise.

Alle:

Du bist Hei - lung, du bist Rat.
You are heal - ing, you are wise.

Liturg   In der Stille sprechen wir unsere Nöte aus
              unsere Sorgen und Mühsale, unsere Ängste und Schatten
              unsere Schuld, unser Versagen
              Gib uns den Mut, Gott, uns zu sehen, wie wir sind

Ch+G   *Du bist Heilung, du bist Rat*

L	Gott Schöpfer / Gott Bewahrerin
G	*Hier bin ich, wie ich bin*
L	Jesus Christus Bruder und Freund
G	*Hier bin ich, wie ich bin*
L	Geist der Weisheit, du Wahrheit und Leben
G	*Hier bin ich, wie ich bin*
Ch+G	*Du bist Heilung, du bist Rat*

6 Langes Schweigen (musikalische Begleitung)

7 Freisprechung

L   Gott, das gütige Ohr der Welt, hört uns
Gott, das liebende Herz der Welt, spricht uns frei
Von Jesus von Nazaret wissen wir
dass Gott die Menschen aus den Dunkelheiten ihrer Seele
aus Schuld und Angst befreien will
Darum spricht Jesus zu dem verachteten Mann am Zoll:
Deine Schuld ist vergeben
Darum spricht Jesus zu der verrufenen Frau:
Deine Schuld ist vergeben.
Amen, ja, so soll es geschehen !

Ch+G   *Du bist Heilung, du bist Rat*

8 Danklied

Kurt Rose   Wolfgang Teichmann: Germany

(Wiederholung 1.Zeile im Kanon / Repeat the first line in canon)

9 Gebet der Freude (vom Liturg gesprochen, von der Gemeinde wiederholt; musikalisch froh begleitet)

L Wir Freigelassnen der Schöpfung
G Wir Freigelassnen der Schöpfung

L sind angekommen aus mühsamem Alltag
G sind angekommen aus mühsamem Alltag

L Jetzt ist uns der Staub
   von der Stirne gewaschen
*G Jetzt ist uns der Staub
   von der Stirne gewaschen*

L Jetzt ist uns die Last
   von der Seele genommen
*G Jetzt ist uns die Last
   von der Seele genommen*

L Jetzt holt uns die Freude
   der Freiheit ein
*G Jetzt holt uns die Freude
   der Freiheit ein*

10 Gloria

Kurt Rose   Wolfgang Teichmann: Germany

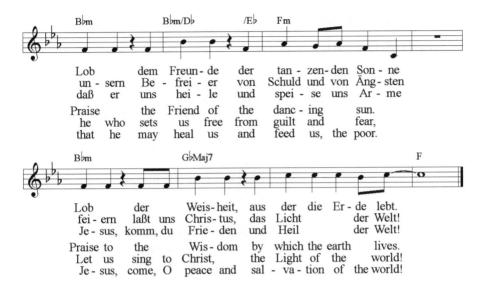

Lob   dem   Freun- de   der   tan - zen- den Son - ne
un - sern Be - frei - er   von   Schuld und von Äng - sten
daß   er   uns   hei - le   und   spei - se uns Ar - me

Praise   the   Friend of   the   danc - ing   sun.
he   who   sets us   free from   guilt and   fear,
that he   may   heal us   and   feed us, the poor.

Lob   der   Weis- heit, aus   der   die Er - de lebt.
fei - ern laßt uns Chris- tus, das Licht   der Welt!
Je - sus, komm, du Frie - den und Heil   der Welt!

Praise to the   Wis- dom   by   which the earth lives.
Let   us   sing to Christ,   the   Light of the   world!
Je - sus, come, O peace and sal - va - tion of the world!

11 Lied der Gemeinde (*ad libitum*, aus dem Gesangbuch)

II. HÖREN UND BEKRÄFTIGEN

12 Sammlung

L   Gott spricht mit uns
    durch die Schöpfung
    durch das Geschehen in der Welt
    durch sein heiliges Wort

    Von Anbeginn war Geselligkeit
    zwischen Schöpfer und Geschöpfen
    lebhaftes Miteinander

    Dem Wort Gottes Einlass zu gewähren
    es in der Seele hörbar werden zu lassen
    halten wir inne
    wir sammeln unsere Sinne und Gedanken
    Schweigen öffnet die Tür
    zum Worte Gottes

G   (verharrt in kurzem Schweigen)

L   Wir hören

13 Lesung

(Ein Bibeltext in zeitgemässer Bearbeitung oder ein anderer geistlicher Text –
Meister Eckehart, Dietrich Bonhoeffer o.ä. – wird zweimal, wenn er kurz genug
ist, dreimal von verschiedenen Stimmen gelesen)

14 Musikalische Meditation der Musikgruppe (Improvisation)

15 Verbale Meditation (Predigt)

16 Glaubensbekenntnis

L   Auf Gottes Anrede in Wort und Ton
    antworten wir mit dem Bekenntnis unseres Glaubens

L/G   *Ich glaube an Gott*
    Schöpfer der Welt und Urheberin des Lebens
    Vater und Mutter aller Geschöpfe
    sorgend für den vielgestaltigen Lauf des Weltalls
    und in ihm des Erdkreises.

    Ich glaube, dass Gott
    den Menschen Jesus von Nazaret ausersehen hat
    das Kommen des Gottesreiches zu verkünden:
    Gerechtigkeit, Frieden und eine gute Schöpfung -
    dass Jesus diese frohe Botschaft gelebt
    und mit dem Tode am Kreuz besiegelt hat
    und dass Gott ihn als unseren Christus
    zu neuem Leben erweckte.

    Ich glaube, dass Gott
    den Geist der Liebe und Versöhnung
    der in Christus Jesus lebt
    für alle Menschen bereithält
    dass dieser Geist uns tröstet
    in den Nöten und Ängsten des Lebens
    und uns antreibt auf Gottes kommende Welt hin
    zu hoffen und zu wirken. Amen

17 Liturgisches Musikstück

Ch   Ich glaube – hilf meinem Unglauben
Alle   *Ich glaube – hilf meinem Unglauben*

18 "Ich möchte glauben"

Kurt Rose   Wolfgang Teichmann: Germany

ich möch-te glau - ben ... oh
ich möch-te glau - ben ... oh
ich möch-te glau - ben ... oh
ich möch-te glau - ben ... oh

I want to be - lieve, ... oh,
I want to be - lieve, ... oh
I want to be - lieve, ... oh,
I want to be - lieve, ... oh,

Chor:

daß Gott den Men - schen än - dern kann
daß Je - sus Freund und Bru - der ist
daß Gott das bun - te Le - ben liebt
daß Je - sus Chris - tus Ant - wort ist

that God can change hu - man be - ings
that Je - sus is our Friend and Brother
that God loves ev - ery kind of life
that Je - sus Christ the an - swer is

und Macht hat ü - ber Haß und Hoch - mut
und Tü - ren hin zur Frei - heit öff - net
in Wäl - dern, Step - pen und in Mee - ren
auf mei - ne Angst auf mei - ne Hoff - nung

has po - wer o - ver hate and pride,
and o - pens up the door to free - dom
in for - ests, steppes and o - ceans wide
to all my fears and all my hopes

ich möch-te glau - ben an den Frie - den der
ich möch-te glau - ben an die Zu - kunft die
ich möch-te glau - ben an die Er - de als
ich möch-te glau - ben an die Freu - de die

I want to be - lieve in the peace that
I want to be - lieve in the fu - ture in
I want to be - lieve in the earth as
I want to be - lieve in the joy that

al - les Den - ken ü - ber-steigt
Welt, die er be - gon - nen hat
Got - tes sehr ge - lieb - tes Kind.
in ihm lebt, die mit ihm kommt.

pass - es all our un - der-standing.
the new world that he be - gan.
God's be - lov - ed, God's own child.
lives in him, and that he brings.

19 Fürbitten

(Diese Fürbitten können und sollen je nach der geistlichen
Richtung des Gottesdienstes formuliert werden. Hier Vorschläge für die
Losung: Versöhnung suchen – Leben gewinnen. Hinweis auf
"Fürbittengebete" in *Neue Texte für den Gottesdienst*, Hannover 1982).

L Gott gütiger Geist
    der in allen Dingen und Wesen
    in allem Werden und Geschehen
    lebt und wirkt –
    vor dir breiten wir unsere Gedanken aus
    unsere Sorgen und Hoffnungen
    für unsere Mitwelt und Umwelt
    und bitten dich um Hilfe:
    Versöhnung zu suchen
    Leben zu gewinnen.

Einzelstimme (E)
    Da sind die vielen Menschen
    deren Zusammenleben gefährdet oder gestört ist
    Eheleute, Eltern und Kinder
    alte Leute in Heimen
    Flüchtlinge in Lagern –
    dass Gott zur Versöhnung helfe
    bitten wir. Wir rufen:
G *Sieh, Gott, unsre Not.*

E Da sind Konflikte
    im politischen und wirtschaftlichen Bereich
    zwischen Arbeitgebern und Arbeitnehmern
    zwischen der Zwei-Drittel-Welt
    und den reichen Ländern
    zwischen Asylanten und Behörden –
    dass Gott zur Gerechtigkeit helfe
    bitten wir. Wir rufen:
G *Sieh, Gott, unsre Not.*

E Da sind die Kinder und Jugendlichen
    in Kriegs- und Krisengebieten
    und auch bei uns
    elternlos, an Leib und Seele misshandelt
    ohne Ausbildung
    einer Sucht verfallen
    sie brauchen materielle und geistliche Zuwendung –
    dass Gott uns zur Hilfe Mut mache
    bitten wir. Wir rufen:
G *Sieh, Gott, unsre Not.*

E   Da ist Gottes gute Schöpfung
    bedroht durch Strahlung und Giftstoffe
    durch Wachstum um jeden Preis
    durch schnelle Nutzung jeder neuen Technologie
    immer grösser wird die Kluft
    zwischen Schöpfung und Mensch –
    dass Gott uns zum Widerstand Mut mache
    damit wir unversehrtes und gesundes Leben
    auf dieser Erde gewinnen
    bitten wir.
    Wir rufen:

G   *Sieh, Gott, unsre Not.*

L   Höre, Gott, wenn wir rufen
    wenn wir fragen:
    wie kann Versöhnung geschehen
    wie können wir Leben gewinnen –
    wir rufen zu dir aus notvollem Herzen:

20 Fürbitt-Litanei

III. TEILEN UND VERBUNDENSEIN

21 Hereinbringen der Gaben

(Zwei Gemeindeglieder tragen in erhobenen Händen einen Korb mit Brot und einen Kelch oder Krug und bringen beides in gemessenen Schritten oder in feierlichem Tanzschritt zum Altar. Dazu entweder improvisierte Musik oder Vorspiel zu 22).

22 Chorlied

Kurt Rose   Wolfgang Teichmann: Germany

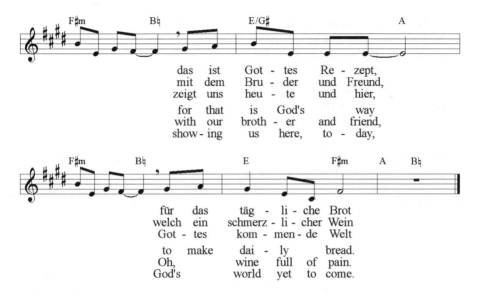

das ist Got - tes Re - zept,
mit dem Bru - der und Freund,
zeigt uns heu - te und hier,

for that is God's way
with our broth - er and friend,
show - ing us here, to - day,

für das täg - li - che Brot
welch ein schmerz - li - cher Wein
Got - tes kom - men - de Welt

to make dai - ly bread.
Oh, wine full of pain.
God's world yet to come.

23 **Dialog** (gesprochen)

E Wann aber kommt
G Wann aber kommt
  Gottes kommende Welt
Ch Beginnt an unserm Tisch, beginnt an unsrer Tür
   wird morgen münden, wird morgen fliessen
   ins Wunder friedvoller Zeit

E Wie aber kommt
G Wie aber kommt
  Gottes kommende Welt
Ch Kommt auf dem Lebenstrom
   und sucht und stürzt und kämpft
   kommt nachts auf klugen Füssen
   kommt tags in pfingstlichen Stürmen
   in Seligpredigt und Heilungsruf

E Wo aber wächst
G Wo aber wächst
  Gottes kommende Welt
Ch Wächst in unserm Innengrund
   und füllt uns Hand und Haus
   wächst gegen die Finsternisse
   wird morgen das Ackerfeld sein
   das Leib und Seele ernährt

24 **Vorrede zum Mahl** – Präfation

L Jetzt ist es am Platze dir, Gott, zu danken –
  die Welt als deine Schöpfung zu erkennen

und deine Wirksamkeit in ihr
hast du uns Seher und Seherinnen
Weise und Heilige geschickt
und schliesslich Jesus von Nazaret
den Menschensohn, den Christus
nun wissen wir von deinem Reich des Friedens
und der Gerechtigkeit, Gott
und wir singen gemeinsam mit allen Geschöpfen
der Erde und des Himmels
deinem Namen Dank und Ehre zu

25 Sanctus

Kurt Rose

Wolfgang Teichmann: Germany

26 Anrufung des Geistes – Epiklese

L Nun lass uns teilhaben, Gott
an deinem lebendigen Geist
lass uns teilhaben an der Gegenwart
unseres Herrn und Bruders Jesus Christus
beim Mahl mit ihm.

Kurt Rose

Wolgang Teichmann: Germany

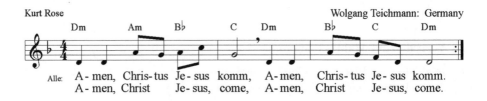

27 Einsetzung

L Unser Bruder Jesus Christus Menschensohn
in der Nacht, da er verraten wurde
nahm er das Brot, dankte und brach's
und gab's seinen Gefährten und Gefährtinnen
und sprach: Nehmt und esst
mein Leib wird für euch gegeben.
Dann nahm er den Kelch
dankte, gab ihnen den und sprach:
Nehmt und trinkt alle daraus
dieser Kelch ist der Liebesbund Gottes
besiegelt durch meinen Tod.
Alles dies tut sooft ihr gemeinsam esst und trinkt
zu meinem Gedächtnis.

G *Amen, Christus Jesus, komm*

28 Gedächtnis-Litanei – Anamnese (dazu Ostinato)

Ch	Zu deinem Gedächtnis, Christus Jesus
G	*Zu deinem Gedächtnis, Christus Jesus*
Ch	Der unser Leben gelebt hat
G	*Der unser Leben gelebt hat*
Ch	Und unseren Tod erlitten
G	*Und unseren Tod erlitten*
Ch	Gegenwärtig als der Lebendige
G	*Gegenwärtig als der Lebendige*
Ch	Damit auch wir leben
G	*Damit auch wir leben*
Ch+G	*Amen, Christus Jesus, komm*

29 Friedensgruss

L Jesus Christus spricht:
Geh hin und versöhne dich
mit deinem Bruder, mit deiner Schwester ehe du kommst.
Geh auf deine Nachbarin, auf deinen Nachbarn zu,
schüttle dem Fremden dort die Hand
es wird ein Zeichen des Friedens
mit hundert anderen Fremden sein.
Sprich ein Wort der Verbundenheit
und du wirst einen Strom der Freundlichkeit öffnen.

(Der Liturg geht auf eine ihm zunächst stehende Person zu und
spricht laut:)
Friede sei mit dir!

(L/Ch/G sind ohne jede Eile eine Zeitlang mit gegenseitigen
Friedenswünschen ringsum im Gottesdienstraum in Bewegung)

30 Vaterunser

31 Austeilung – Kommunion

L   Kommt
             es ist alles bereit
             Brot und Wein
             Versöhnung und Friede

L+EE   *Das Brot, das wir brechen*
             ist die Gemeinschaft
             mit unserm Bruder und Herrn Jesus Christus

             Der Wein, den wir trinken
             ist die Gemeinschaft
             mit unserm Bruder und Herrn Jesus Christus

IV. DANKEN, SEGNEN UND SENDEN

32 Dankgebet

L   Wir sagen Gott Dank dafür
             dass er uns freundlich bedient hat
             ein solches Mahl
             gibt uns Mut und Kraft
             unser Leben zu bestehen

Ch+G

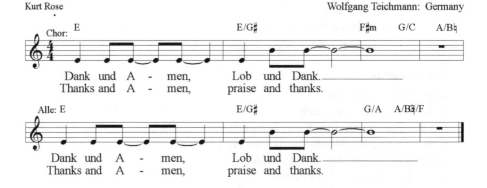

Kurt Rose   Wolfgang Teichmann: Germany

Chor:
Dank und A - men,   Lob und Dank.
Thanks and A - men,   praise and thanks.

Alle:
Dank und A - men,   Lob und Dank.
Thanks and A - men,   praise and thanks.

L/E   Wir danken dir, Christus Jesus
             dass du gegenwärtig bist in unserm Leben
             und wir mit deiner Hilfe
             als versöhnte Menschen
             miteinander umzugehen wissen
             in Gerechtigkeit und Frieden

Ch+G   *Dank und Amen, Lob und Dank*

L/E   Wir danken dir, heiliger Geist
           dass du uns drängst
           mit der guten Schöpfung Gottes
           liebevoll zusammenzuleben

Ch+G   *Dank und Amen, Lob und Dank*

L/E   Wir danken dir, Gott
           dass du uns deine kommende Welt
           in der Botschaft und durch das Leben Jesu
           sichtbar und greifbar aufgezeigt hast –
           hilf uns seinem Beispiel zu folgen
           zu hören und zu handeln
           zum Glück und Segen der Menschen
           und zu deiner Freude

Ch+G   *Dank und Amen, Lob und Dank*

33 "Wenn nun auch wir"

Kurt Rose   Wolgang Teichmann: Germany

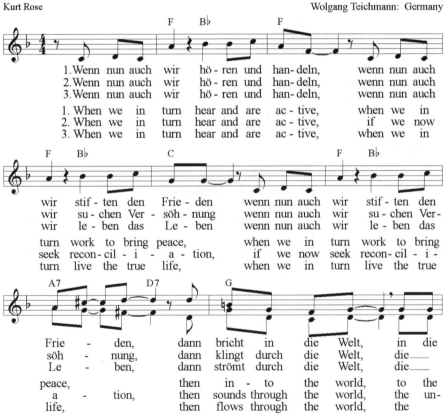

1. Wenn nun auch wir hö-ren und han-deln, wenn nun auch
2. Wenn nun auch wir hö-ren und han-deln, wenn nun auch
3. Wenn nun auch wir hö-ren und han-deln, wenn nun auch

1. When we in turn hear and are ac-tive, when we in
2. When we in turn hear and are ac-tive, if we now
3. When we in turn hear and are ac-tive, when we in

wir stif-ten den Frie-den wenn nun auch wir stif-ten den
wir su-chen Ver-söh-nung wenn nun auch wir su-chen Ver-
wir le-ben das Le-ben wenn nun auch wir le-ben das

turn work to bring peace, when we in turn work to bring
seek recon-cil-i-a-tion, if we now seek recon-cil-i-
turn live the true life, when we in turn live the true

Frie-den, dann bricht in die Welt, in die
söh-nung, dann klingt durch die Welt, die___
Le-ben, dann strömt durch die Welt, die___

peace, then in-to the world, to the
a-tion, then sounds through the world, the un-
life, then flows through the world, the

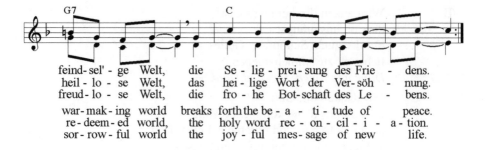

feind-sel'-ge Welt, die Se-lig-prei-sung des Frie - dens.
heil-lo-se Welt, das hei-lige Wort der Ver-söh - nung.
freud-lo-se Welt, die fro-he Bot-schaft des Le - bens.

war-mak-ing world breaks forth the be-a-ti-tude of peace.
re-deem-ed world, the holy word rec-on-cil-i-a-tion.
sor-row-ful world the joy-ful mes-sage of new life.

34 Sendungswort

L   Wir sind bei Jesus Christus zu Gast gewesen
wir haben Gottes gute Gaben empfangen
nun gehen wir hin in unsere Wohnungen
zu unseren Mitmenschen, an unsere Arbeit
ausgestattet, Jesu Wort und Wesen
in die Tat umzusetzen
Salz der Erde
Licht der Welt zu werden
Gerechtigkeit zu suchen
Frieden zu stiften
die Schöpfung zu bewahren
und so Leben zu gewinnen

Ch+G   *Dank und Amen, Lob und Dank*

35 Segen

L   Gott, der Schöpfer der Welt, segne uns
Gott, die Bewahrerin des Lebens, behüte uns
heute und allezeit

Ch+G   *Dank und Amen, Lob und Dank*

36 Schlusslied der Gemeinde (s.o. Nr. 4)

A Mass for Our Time

KURT ROSE AND WOLFGANG TEICHMANN

For the music, please see the German text, pp. 98-114.

I. ARRIVAL AND SETTING UP

1 Entrance music

2 Invitation

3 Brief musical introduction to the hymn

4 Hymn: Place in which life is born

5 Our situation

Leader	We turn to God God the indwelling power that reaches around the world
	Open our eyes, God so that we see who we are You see where people are going even if we fly up to heaven you are there with us even if we hide in the night Give us the courage, God, to see ourselves as we are.
Response	*You are healing*
Choir	You are healing, you are wise.
Congregation	*You are healing, You are wise.*
L.	In the silence we tell our troubles our worries and struggles our fears and dark places our guilt, our failures. Give us the courage, God, to see ourselves as we are.

• Original German. Text Kurt Rose; music Wolfgang Teichmann 1995-97; English Isabel and Tom Best, Dagmar Heller, Terry MacArthur, 1997.

CCh.	*You are healing, you are healing.*
L.	God-Creator, God-Protectress:
C.	*Here I am, just as I am*
L.	Jesus Christ, brother and friend:
C.	*Here I am, just as I am*
L.	Spirit of wisdom, you who are truth and life:
C.	*Here I am, just as I am.*
CCh.	*You are healing, You are healing.*

6 Long silence (with music)

7 Declaration of pardon

L.	God, the kindest ear in the world, hears us,
	God, the loving heart of the word, pardons us,
	From Jesus of Nazareth we have learned
	God wants to free people from the darkness of their souls,
	from the bondage of guilt and fear.
	Therefore Jesus says to the despised man collecting taxes:
	Your sin is forgiven.
	Therefore Jesus says to the woman with a ruined reputation:
	Your sin is forgiven.
	Amen, yes, so be it!
CCh.	*You are healing, You are healing.*

8 Hymn of thanksgiving

9 Litany of joy

(Spoken by the leader, echoed by the congregation,
accompanied by joyful music)

L. We are creatures set free
C. We are creatures set free

L. who have come from our daily struggle
C. who have come from our daily struggle

L. Now the dust is wiped away from our foreheads
C. now the dust is wiped away from our foreheads

L. Now the burdens are lifted from our souls
C. Now the burdens are lifted from our souls

L. Now the joy of freedom catches up with us
C. Now the joy of freedom catches up with us.

10 Gloria (sung)

11 Congregational hymn (from a familiar hymnal)

II. Hearing and Confirming

12 Centring prayer

L. God talks with us
through the creation
through what happens in the world
through God's holy word

From the beginning there has been
companionship between Creator and creatures,
a warm and lively togetherness

To let God's word enter,
to let it be heard within us
we sit still
and gather up our thoughts and feelings
Silence opens the door
to God's word.

C. (brief silence)

L. We are listening

13 Reading

(Text from the Bible in contemporary language, or another spiritual text, for example from Meister Eckhart, Dietrich Bonhoeffer, and so on. Read twice or, if it is very short, three times by different voices)

14 Meditation in music (impromptu)

15 Meditation in words (sermon)

16 Confession of faith

L. God has called us in words and music.
We answer
confessing our faith.

L/C. I believe in God
Creator of the world and womb of life
Father and Mother of all creatures
who cares for the many-orbited universe
and within it, the earth.

I believe that God
elected the human being Jesus of Nazareth
to announce the coming of God's reign
of justice, peace and a good creation,
that Jesus lived this joyful news
and sealed it with his death on the cross
and that God raised him as our Christ
to new life.

> I believe that God
> offers to all human beings
> the Spirit of love and reconciliation
> which lives in Christ Jesus,
> that this Spirit comforts us
> in our troubles and fears
> and spurs us on
> to hope and to work
> for God's world to come.
> Amen.

17 Musical response

Choir   I believe – help my unbelief.
Congregation I believe – help my unbelief.

18 Hymn: I Want to Believe

19 Intercessions

(These prayers may, and should, be composed especially for each particular worship service. Those given here were offered for the theme "Seeking reconciliation – finding life")

L. God, kind Spirit
   living and working in all things and beings
   in all becomings and happenings –
   we lift up before you our thoughts,
   our sorrows, our hopes
   for our world near and far
   and we ask your help
   to be reconciled and to find life.

A single voice (V)
   There are the many people
   whose life together is threatened or troubled,
   married couples, parents and children,
   elderly people in homes,
   refugees in camps –
   that they may be helped to find reconciliation
   we pray and call upon God.

C. God, look upon our need.

V. There are political and economic conflicts
   between employers and employees
   between the two-thirds world
   and the rich countries
   between asylum-seekers and those in authority –

that they may be helped to find justice
we pray and call upon God.

C. *God, look upon our need.*

V. There are children and youths
in regions of war and crisis
and also here among us
orphaned, without education,
abused in body and soul,
in bondage to an addiction
who need material and spiritual caring –
that we may be given the courage to help
we pray and call upon God.

C. *God, look upon our need.*

V. There is God's good creation
endangered by radiation and poisons,
by growth at any price,
by the rush to exploit every new technology,
and the gap keeps on widening
between creation and human beings –
for courage to offer resistance
that we may regain a whole and healthy life
on this earth
we pray and call upon God.

C. *God, look upon our need*

L. Hear us God, when we call
when we ask
how can reconciliation happen
how can we find life –
we call to you with hearts full of sorrow.

20 Litany of intercession (sung)

III. SHARING AND BELONGING TOGETHER

21 The bringing of gifts

(Two members of the congregation carry in a basket with bread and a cup or pitcher. They hold the elements high and walk with measured steps, or dance reverently, to the altar, accompanied by music – impromptu or introducing the next hymn.)

22 Hymn: Bread and wine

23 Dialogue

(Spoken by a single voice [V], congregation [C] and choir [Ch])

V. When will it come
C. *When will it come*
    God's new world?
Ch. It begins at our table
    It begins at our door
    it will gather tomorrow
    it will flow tomorrow
    into the miracle of peacetime.

V. How does it come
C. *How does it come*
    God's new world?
Ch. It comes on the stream of life
    seeking, rushing, struggling,
    comes by night with wise footsteps
    comes by day in Pentecostal storms
    in preaching of blessedness and call to healing.

V. Where does it grow
C. *Where does it grow*
    God's new world?
Ch. It grows deep within us
    and fills our hands and house
    grows in spite of all darkness
    will be tomorrow the harvest field
    to feed our bodies and souls.

24 Words before the meal – preface

L. Now is the time and place
   to say thank you, God,
   to recognize this world as your creation
   and your potency within it.
   That we might know you
   you sent at first
   prophets, wise and holy men and women,
   and finally Jesus of Nazareth
   the Son of Man, Christ.
   Now we know about your reign of peace
   and of justice, O God, and we sing
   together with all creatures
   and earth and heaven
   thanks and honour to your name.

25 Sanctus: Beautiful and wondrous (sung)

26 Calling upon the Holy Spirit – Epiclesis

L.   O God, may we share
                in your living Spirit
                may we share in the presence
                of our Lord and brother Jesus Christ
                at the meal with him.

CCh   *Amen. Christ Jesus, come.* (sung twice)

27 Dedication

L. Our brother Jesus Christ, Son of Man
    in the night in which he was betrayed
    took bread, gave thanks and broke it
    and gave it to his companions
    and said: Take and eat
    my body is given for you.
    Then he took the cup,
    gave thanks, gave it to them and said:
    Take and drink, all of you,
    this cup is the covenant of love with God
    sealed by my death.
    Do all of this
    as often as you eat and drink together
    in remembrance of me.

C. *Amen. Christ Jesus, come.*

28 Litany of remembrance – Anamnesis

(Accompanied by ostinato)

Choir   In remembrance of you, Christ Jesus.
Congregation *In remembrance of you, Christ Jesus.*

Ch.   who lived our life
C.   *who lived our life*

Ch.   and suffered our death
C.   *and suffered our death*

Ch.   and are present, the Living One
C.   *and are present, the Living One*

Ch.   that we may live.
C.   *that we may live.*

Ch. and C.   *Amen. Christ Jesus, come.*

29 Passing of the peace

L. Jesus Christ says:
    Go and be reconciled
    with your brother and with your sister

before you come.
Go to your neighbour
shake hands with the stranger,
it will be a sign of peace made
with a hundred other strangers.
Speak a sympathetic word
and you will release a torrent of friendliness.

(The leader goes to someone standing near him
and says aloud:)
Peace be with you!
C. *And also with you.*

(Time is allowed for the congregation, choir and leader to move about the room
unhurriedly and exchange a greeting of peace)

30 The Lord's prayer

31 Communion

L.   Come, for all is ready,
            bread and wine,
            peace and reconciliation.

(V)   The bread which we break
            is the communion with our brother Jesus Christ.

(V)   The wine which we drink
            is the communion with our brother Jesus Christ.

IV. THANKSGIVING, BLESSING AND SENDING FORTH

32 Prayer of thanksgiving

L.   We give thanks to God
            whose kindness has fed us at this table
            such a meal gives us courage and strength
            to keep living our lives.

Ch.   *Thanks and Amen, praise and thanks.* (sung twice)

L.   We thank you, Christ Jesus
            that you are present in our lives
            and that with your help
            we know how to live
            as people reconciled with one another
            in justice and peace.

CCh.   *Thanks and Amen...*

L.   We thank you, Holy Spirit
            that you spur us on

	to live lovingly with God's good creation.
CCh.	*Thanks and Amen...*
L.	We thank you, God
	that in Jesus' message, and through his life,
	you have let us see and touch your world to come.
	Help us to follow his example
	to listen and to act
	to bring happiness and blessing to all people
	and joy to you
C.	*Thanks and Amen...*

33 Hymn: When We in Turn (sung by the choir)

34 Sending forth

L.	We have been guests of Jesus Christ
	we have received God's good gifts.
	Now we go to our homes,
	to our neighbours, to our work
	equipped to put Jesus' words and being into action
	to be salt of the earth,
	light of the world,
	to seek justice
	to make peace
	to preserve the creation
	to gain life.
CCh.	*Thanks and Amen...*

35 Blessing

L.	May God, the Creator of the world, bless us,
	May God, the Protectress of life, keep us
	today and for all time.
CCh.	*Thanks and Amen...*

36 Closing congregational hymn (see no. 4 above)

Materials for Eucharistic Services

1. Eucharistic Prayers

1 Sursum corda

PREFACE

SANCTUS

Leader	In a world of longing, in work, in play and rest, in creative power and visions
All	*You are here, God, in Christ our Saviour.*
Leader	In a world of disorder, in suffering, sorrow and struggle, in marginalization and powerlessness,
All	*You are here, God, in Christ our Redeemer.*
Leader	In the church, your body, in life, death and resurrection, in signs of renewal and unity,
All	*You are here, God, in Christ our Intercessor.*
Leader	In a world of hunger, in bread and wine, in prayer and unity,
All	*You are here, God, in Christ, the bread of life.*
Leader	The night he was betrayed
Leader	You sent your Son to save the world.
All	*We thank you, God.*
Leader	You send your Holy Spirit upon these holy gifts and upon our community
All	*We praise you, God.*
Leader	You send us out in service of your kingdom.
All	*We bless you, God.*

(Per Harling)

2 Sursum corda

PREFACE

Leader	It is indeed right to praise and glorify your Being.

You are the beginning and the end,
the source of all life, beyond all time and space.
In thankfulness and in unity
we join the everlasting song,
the song of all ages, the song of the angels,
the song with all who glorify your name
on earth as in heaven:
Sanctus Holy, holy, holy

Leader   For the wonders of creation,
         for the ripening of the grapes,
         for the growing of the seed
All   *We praise you, Father, Son and Holy Spirit!*

Leader   For the salvation in Jesus Christ,
         for his life, death and resurrection,
         for his presence in this bread and wine
All   *We praise you, Father, Son and Holy Spirit!*

Leader   For the descent of the Holy Spirit
         upon our assembly and upon these gifts,
         for the unity in your love,
All   *We praise you, Father, Son and Holy Spirit!*

Leader   For the faithful of the past,
         for those who now follow you,
         for those who will come,
All   *We praise you, Father, Son and Holy Spirit!*

Leader   The night, when Jesus Christ was betrayed, he...

PRAYER OF THANKSGIVING

Leader   We have received bread and wine,
         the body and the blood of your Son, Jesus Christ.
All   *We thank you, Lord.*

Leader   We have shared your living Word
         in reflection and prayer, in faith and hope.
All   *We bless you, Lord.*

Leader   We have been singing your glory
         with body, mind and spirit before your face.
All   *We praise you, Lord.*
         Amen.

                                        (Per Harling)

2. Eucharistic Prayer on the Theme of Justice

Leader   Blessed are you, strong and faithful God.
              You gave us breath and speech,
              that all the living
              might find a voice to sing your praise,
              and to celebrate the creation you call good.
              So now, with all the powers of heaven and earth
              We sing the ageless hymn of your glory:
              Sanctus Holy, holy, holy...

Leader   All holy God,
              how wonderful is the work of your hands!
              When sin had scarred the world,
              you entered into covenant to renew the whole creation.

              As a mother tenderly gathers her children,
              as a father joyfully welcomes his own,
              you embraced a people as your own,
              and filled them with longing
              for a peace that would last
              and for a justice that would never fail.

              Through countless generations
              your people hungered for the bread of freedom.
              From them you raised up Jesus, your Son,
              the living bread, in whom ancient hungers are satisfied.
              He healed the sick,
              though He himself would suffer;
              He offered life to sinners,
              though death would hunt him down.
              But with a love stronger than death,
              He opened wide his arms
              and surrendered his spirit.

              On the night before He met with death,
              Jesus came to the table with those He loved.
              He took bread and praised you, God of all creation.
              He broke the bread among his disciples and said:
              Take this, all of you, and eat it.
              This is my body, given for you.

              When the supper was ended,
              He took the cup of wine
              and gave thanks to you, God of all creation.
              He passed the cup among his disciples and said:
              Take this, all of you, and drink from it.
              This is the cup of the new covenant sealed in my blood
              for the forgiveness of sin.
              Do this in remembrance of me.

People	*Gracious God,*
	As we offer for you our sacrifice of praise and thanksgiving,
	we commemorate Jesus, your Son.
	Death could not bind him,
	for you raised him up in the Spirit of holiness
	and exalted him as Lord of creation.

Leader   Great is the mystery of faith:

People   *Christ has died,*
Christ has risen,
Christ will come again.

Leader   Eternal God,
let your Holy Spirit move in power over us
and over these earthly gifts of bread and wine,
that they may be the communion of the body
and the blood of Christ,
and that we may become one in him.
May this coming in glory find us
ever watchful in prayer,
strong in truth and love,
and faithful in the breaking of the bread.

Then, at last, all people will be free,
all divisions healed,
and with your whole creation,
we will sing your praise,
through your Son, Jesus Christ.

Through Christ, with Christ, in Christ,
in the unity of the Holy Spirit,
all glory and honour are yours, almighty God,
forever and ever.

People   *Amen.*
...

BLESSING AND SENDING

Leader   Use us, O God, to set the pillars of justice
on which alone real security and peace can be built:

People   *Use us that the sick may be healed, the disabled empowered,*
the prisoners freed, the blind restored to sight.
Use us that the hungry may be fed,
the unproductive made useful,
the dispossessed defended, the outcast welcomed.

Leader   Into the world of brokenness and strife, go forth as new persons in
Christ who is the Bread of Life.

(Prepared by a group at the meeting)

3. From a Mass on the Theme of Creation and the Environment

Invocation

Leader Praise to you, Creator of heaven and earth.
All *You give us the food of the earth and the water of the well.*

Leader Praise to you, Jesus Christ, who have walked our ways.
All *You have made the holiness of the earth obvious to us.*

Leader Praise to you, Holy Spirit, Lifegiver and Helper.
All *You arouse our song of praise in faith and struggle.*

Prayer of confession

Leader Creator and Life-giver,
we are part of your beautiful
but fragile creation.
We have the responsibility to protect,
to nurture and to respect it.
We have failed in our responsibility.
Therefore we cry:
All *Kyrie eleison...* (sung)

Leader The earth is our mother,
our origin, our nourishment.
Every seed in the depth of the earth
vibrates with your creating will.
When the earth is spoiled and poisoned
by greed and short-range interests,
we deny our origin,
we suppress your will.
Therefore we cry:
All *Kyrie eleison...* (sung)

Leader The earth is a water planet.
The seas are our amniotic fluid.
All life carries your creative water;
people, vegetation and animals.
When the water is polluted
it reacts against us and our future.
Therefore we cry:
All *Kyrie eleison...* (sung)

Leader The air is the breath of life,
the breathing-space of the earth.
Every breath is a reminder
of your creative force.
When the air is polluted
the lungs of the earth are damaged

and your strength is suppressed.
Therefore we cry:

All   *Kyrie eleison...* (sung)

Silence

Words of forgiveness

Leader   Jesus Christ who joins the Creator with creation,
has heard your groaning and cleanses you from all guilt.
Arise and walk in faith and struggle
for the integrity of creation.
In the name of the Creator, the Redeemer and the Lifegiver.
Amen.

(Per Harling)

4. Other Materials for Worship in Ecumenical Contexts

Calls to worship/invocations

1

(An unlit candle is brought to the front.)

Leader   In the beginning was the Word
and the Word was with God
and the Word was God.

All   *What has come into being in him was life,*
and the life was the light of all people.

(The candle is lit. During the singing a cross is brought to the front)

Hallelujah...

Leader   And the Word became flesh
and lived among us.

All   *And we have seen his glory,*
the glory as of a father's only son,
full of grace and truth.

Hallelujah...

(During the singing a Bible is brought to the front.)

Leader   Let the word of Christ dwell in you richly;
teach and admonish one another in all wisdom.

All	*Sanctify us in the truth;* *your word is truth.*
	Hallelujah...

(Per Harling)

2

Leader	We have come together
All	*with our longing,* *with our faith and our doubts.*
Leader	We have come together
All	*seeking the depths of faith* *in prayer and praise.*
Leader	We have come together
All	*to share, to learn, to grow* *in unity and in the love of God.*
Leader	Let us be silent before the face of God.

(Per Harling)

Confessions of sin

1

Leader	Lord, you surround us with your blessings. Take away everything that prevents us from following you. Blessed are the poor in the spirit.
All	*Open ourselves to your kingdom.*
Leader	Blessed are the meek.
All	*Forgive our lack of meekness.*
Leader	Blessed are the merciful.
All	*Forgive our lack of mercy.*
Leader	Blessed are the pure in heart.
All	*Give us pure hearts* *in your mercy and forgiveness.*

(Per Harling)

2

(After this prayer is used, people should be invited to come forward to light candles, praying individually...)

Leader	Lord, we entrust ourselves and our world to you, and we pray:
All	*When the darkness of our doubts surrounds us,* *help us to light the lights of faith.* *When the darkness of our despair surrounds us,*

help us to light the lights of hope.
When the darkness of our indifference surrounds us,
help us to light the lights of love.
Let your light shine through us,
release us, cleanse us, forgive us.

WORDS OF FORGIVENESS

Leader   (holds a candle in his/her hand)
           In the name of Jesus Christ, the light of the world:
           You are forgiven and released.
           "Arise, shine; for your light has come,
           and the glory of the Lord has risen upon you."

(Per Harling)

3

Leader   We belong together
All   *like members in one body.*

Leader   When there is dissension within the body,
All   *Lord, have mercy on us.*

           Kyrie eleison...(sung)

Leader   If one member suffers,
All   *all suffer together with it.*

Leader   When we lack compassion,
All   *Lord, have mercy on us.*

           Kyrie eleison... (sung)

Leader   If one member is honoured,
All   *all rejoice together with it.*

Leader   When we lack thankfulness and shared joy,
All   *Lord, have mercy on us.*

           Kyrie eleison... (sung)

Leader   We belong together,
All   *like members in one body.*

WORDS OF FORGIVENESS

Leader   On behalf of Jesus Christ, our Saviour,
           I assure you:
           You are forgiven, forgive others.
           You are restored, restore others.
           You are reconciled with God, be reconciled with others,
           in the name of the Father, the Son and the Holy Spirit.
           Amen.

(Per Harling)

Blessings and words of sending

1

Leader	Blessings from God who creates and carries life who loves and struggles who renews and gives life. May God surround you with rest and comfort and challenge your creativeness and ability in the name of the Father, the Son and the Holy Spirit. Amen.

2

Leader	May God bless us/you with a mind of sensitivity, with a heart of tenderness, with a strength of truth, in the name of God, the Creator, Jesus Christ, the Saviour, and the Holy Sprit, the Life-giver. Amen.

3

Leader	Let us walk with faith
All	*where there is doubt.*
Leader	Let us walk with hope
All	*where there is despair.*
Leader	Let us walk with love
All	*where there is hate.*
Leader	Let us walk with God
All	*in the name of Jesus Christ, our Lord.*

4

Leader	Blessed are those who hunger and thirst for righteousness.
All	*They will be filled.*
Leader	Blessed are the merciful.
All	*They will receive mercy.*
Leader	Blessed are the peacemakers.
All	*They will be called children of God.*
Leader	Walk with righteous hearts, merciful hands and peaceful minds.
All	*Amen.*

5

Leader	The God of blessings is a child in a cradle.
All	*Give us strength to give the children a future.*
Leader	The God of blessings has wounded hands.
All	*Give us courage to be vulnerable.*
Leader	The God of blessings is the way, the truth and the life.
All	*Give us strength to walk the way of truth.*

6

Leader   We may leave our worship
with faith in our hearts,
with a song of praise on our lips,
with love in our minds
and with caring in our hands.
Go in peace.

(Per Harling)

Affirmations about Worship in Ecumenical Contexts

ROBERT GRIBBEN

The Lima liturgy seminar at Bossey in May 1995 was not constituted as a decision-making body, yet several of the participants had been part of the Faith and Order consultation at Ditchingham in 1994, and others had had equal experience in the fields of ecumenical liturgical theology and practice. A number of the texts produced were in fact shared with the whole group, and improved thereby, but the written material from the seminar does not carry the formal assent of the whole company. What follows are the reflections of one participant, thinking somewhat laterally, as it were, about affirmations which were emerging from the larger discussion, and ancillary to a more considered document on the common *ordo* which built on the Ditchingham consultation.

Jesus Christ, who is High Priest and Lord, unites in his own liturgy the life of the world and the glory of God.
Our meeting at Bossey ended in the week of the feast of the Ascension. Christ Jesus has entered into the holy place. There he – he, the incarnate One, the One who knows our human life and death – intercedes for us. That is how our human cries are heard at the right hand of God. Through the Spirit, those who by baptism are "in Christ Jesus" pray to the Father, and find themselves caught up into the communion at the heart of God the holy Trinity. From this same source comes, as grace upon grace, all that the world needs for fullness of life.

We, who so easily separate liturgy and life, are humbled by this sign of the all-embracing grace of God. We, who find it difficult to be both caught up in the spirit of worship and immersed in the struggle for justice and peace, discover that the ascended Lord has brought together what we have separated. The knowledge that God knows the life of humanity in Jesus, and hears the cries of our world in the voice of Jesus, moves us to "take the shoes from our feet". Mystery is encountered in the love of God, and leads to praise, penitence, pardon, listening to the living Word, and responding in faith, in further prayer, and in gifts for the poor. This mystery of God's love leads us to the table, to thanksgiving and eating and drinking together, and again to mission in Christ's way in the world. We need, then, to hold together in our worship the wonder of God's love for the entire cosmos in Jesus Christ and the wonder that God is already at work healing the pain and suffering in the world. Liturgy places us at the heart of the work of God.

We have discovered that the needs of the world are not left outside the liturgy; in the liturgy, the sin and needs of the world are present through the crucified and

living One, and through the people of God, and are brought to the place of healing, the place where God is worshipped.

We were led to meditate on our high calling in Christ Jesus, both to offer
through him our prayers for the life of the world, and to offer ourselves in him for
the life of the world. And then we may discover truly that the closer we draw to
Christ, the closer we shall find ourselves to each other.

Liturgy has a shape and a dynamic; it is more than a text.

We have also observed the "flow" of the liturgy, its internal logic and dynamic.
This dynamic may be observed in many encounters with God recorded in scripture: Moses at the burning bush (Ex. 3:1-6), Jacob at Peniel (Gen. 32:30), Isaiah
in the temple (Isa. 6:6-13), Mary before Gabriel (Luke 1:26-38). Here are common elements of adoration, a sense of sinfulness, the experience of acceptance by
God, and a call to obedience. But these elements do not occur in isolation or by
accident. Adoration, confession and assurance lead to mission. Or, as we have
noted in the ancient *ordo* of the church, the reading and proclamation of the word
leads us to pray for the world and to offer our intercessions and our gifts; the
thanksgiving at the table and the shared meal impel us to renewed mission
together with our missionary God. Part of the renewal of our worship will be to
tune our ears to this powerful pattern, and to find the words and actions which best
express it.

Worship is local. An ecumenical gathering is also local.

Our conversations at Bossey have revealed to many of us how limited is our
experience of worship. Each of us has come from a particular place, both bound
and inspired by particular cultures and histories. As we have listened to ways of
praying other than our own, we have encountered both the familiar and the strange
and new. Many insights have been gained for reuse and reinterpretation in our own
contexts. We find ourselves challenged to work with our congregations at home,
to bring them into the experience and discussion we have had here, and thus to
continue the exploration – because liturgy is always local.

But we have also discovered a new context: a gathering of Christians from
many places into one place, an hospitable environment on the shores of Lake
Geneva, where we have shared our faith and found ourselves called to worship
together. This worship, too, is local. It represents the world in a way not usually
open to any of us, but we are a single community, already one in Christ – in baptism, in the gift of word and prayer, and drawn to the one table where we are as
yet constrained by the competing demands of love and truth. The challenge of
"ecumenical worship" is, thus, before us as a reality. It is simply not good enough
to "do someone else's prayer". What we offer must be the prayer of *this* community – and, we were aware – of every gathering from across denominational and
cultural boundaries wherever they occur around the contemporary world. We were
able to share many different traditions of prayer, and enter into them in the Spirit,
and this was good; but so much is now the common possession of the churches
that we found ourselves able to share at a deeper level, and desiring to go deeper
still.

Our ecumenical experience and mutual learning during this half century have brought us to a new place, where the churches find themselves experiencing such profound commonality of faith and worship that their relationship to each other at the Lord's table needs to be considered anew.

We find ourselves facing the question: What is the significance of this common possession, both at the deepest level of the *ordo*, and of so much else in text, music and symbol? What is the *ecclesial* significance of this possession?

At Ditchingham, the consultation noted:

> Certainly the ecumenical movement has moved on in the last fifty years or so from simply inviting fellow-Christians to attend the characteristic celebration of a particular host church. The confessional element remains, of course, in that the presider or president of the liturgy must have the authority of a particular church, and on that the participation of others depends. At the end of this ecumenical century, however, such presiders on ecumenical occasions, while they may use some elements distinctive of their own tradition, will also likely draw on the large pool of liturgical and musical resources which are now accepted across the churches (and nations and cultures). This is a new relationship between the confessional and the ecumenical in prayer and worship.[1]

Have we, therefore, begun to move into a new ecumenical situation, one which requires us to ask again what "church" is, to search the limits of our received definitions? Through the experience of the ecumenical and liturgical movements, have the churches come to a point where they must ask again whether they may now meet at the one table? Or are there particular moments in their life together, such as meetings for the deliberate purpose of fostering unity in Christ, when sufficient signs of their being the catholic church in one place at one time are present that they may break the bread together?

Inculturation is a special force for local unity, and has posed the ecumenical questions in new ways.

Time and time again, we found that the recovery of local cultures broke down the barriers which history had placed between local peoples. We observed this phenomenon amongst ourselves, as we saw the unity of those who came from a sufficiently common culture – the Latin American or the African, for instance – a unity which freed them in these moments from the received traditions of Europe or America. We are experiencing a new form of unity in this cultural rediscovery, and it holds the potential to challenge the universal "unity" which particular denominational or confessional bodies have supplied in the past.

Much more can be said on the complex issues of inculturation and its relationship to contextualization, but these are not the concern of this reflection. One key point calls for notice.

As Fr Anscar Chupungco noted in his paper "Liturgical Inculturation and the Search for Unity" at Ditchingham:

> When people speak of the liturgy of the Roman Catholic Church, the Anglican communion, or the Reformed churches, they normally refer to the practices, however loosely observed, that hold these churches together and distinguish them from each other. It is not unusual that the founding church from Europe or North America hands

on its liturgy, which is identifiably Western, to the new church in Africa, Latin America or Asia. Thus both mother and daughter churches normally share the same cultural tradition in worship. But when a daughter church inculturates its liturgy, will unity with the mother church not become less evident? On the other hand, will it not come about that in the same country or region the resemblance among local churches belonging to different confessions will be closer because they share a common cultural expression?[2]

Our brief experience of this potential was very positive. It is of great importance in the search for unity that the churches note this movement and ask again what it means for the search for unity "in one place".

Doxology and diakonia are one. Our praise of God and our work for the kingdom are united both in the liturgy and in "the liturgy after the liturgy".

"Blessed is the kingdom of the Father and of the Son and of the Holy Spirit; now and for ever, world without end. Amen."

So begins the ancient liturgy of St John Chrysostom. In the very opening words of the liturgy, the great hope of the people of God is expressed: "Your kingdom come; your will be done on earth as in heaven." We have been incorporated into this hope by baptism; we have seen the reign of God in our lives; we wait for its final realization at the end of the ages. It is a profound mystery that this doxology, this pure praise of God, should also contain all our intercession, our longing for the rule of God.

Likewise, the dismissal, the final words of the liturgy, express the transformation which has occurred there once more: because we have listened to the word of God read and proclaimed, because we have given thanks at the table and shared the body and blood of Christ in the meal, we find ourselves caught up in the active life of the Father, through the Son, in the Spirit, working for the reconciliation of all things in the unity of the one God, to whom be glory for ever and ever. Amen.

NOTES

[1] Report of the consultation, in *So We Believe, So We Pray,* Faith and Order paper no. 171, Thomas F. Best and Dagmar Heller, eds, Geneva, WCC, 1995, p.22.
[2] *Ibid.*, pp.55-56.

IV

Material for Reflection on the Structure and Content of the Eucharistic Service

This collection of ancient and contemporary texts in official use in various churches takes up the two proposals made at the end of Gordon Lathrop's paper (1) that we focus on the *shape* of the eucharistic service, as a resource for the churches' common confession and life; and (2) that we share ancient and contemporary *eucharistic texts* central to the churches' liturgical practice today, as a resource for their common worship and for their liturgical and theological reflection on the meaning and administration of the eucharist today. The following texts may be read in association with the Lima liturgy.

Foundations
for the Christian Assembly

From the earliest days of the church, Christian worship has been marked by a pattern of gathering, word, meal and sending. These basic elements – rooted in the New Testament, revealed in the writings of the early church, and reflected, for example, in the Lutheran confessions and ecumenical documents – constitute the centre of the church's worship.

* * *

Beginning with Moses and all the prophets, Jesus interpreted to them the things about himself in all the scriptures... When he was at the table with them, he took bread, blessed and broke it, and gave it to them. Then their eyes were opened and they recognized him.

Luke 24:27,30-31a

The baptized devoted themselves to the apostles' teaching and fellowship, to the breaking of bread and the prayers.

Acts 2:42

On Sunday all are gathered together in unity. The records of the apostles or the writings of the prophets are read for as long as time allows. The presider exhorts and invites us into the pattern of these good things. Then we all stand and offer prayer.

When we have concluded the prayer, bread is set out together with wine... The presider then offers prayer and thanksgiving and the people sing out their assent, saying the "Amen". There is a distribution of the things over which thanks has been said and each person participates, and these things are sent to those who are not present.

Those who are prosperous give what they wish according to each one's own choice, and the collection is deposited with the presider, who aids orphans and widows, those in want because of disease, those in prison, and foreigners who are staying here.

We hold this meeting together on Sunday since it is the first day on which God, having transformed darkness and matter, created the world. On the same day Jesus Christ our Saviour rose from the dead. On Sunday he appeared to his apostles and disciples and taught them these things which we present to you.

From the Apology of Justin Martyr (c.150 AD)

It is taught among us that one holy Christian church will be and remain forever. This is the assembly of all believers among whom the gospel is preached in its purity and the holy sacraments are administered according to the gospel.

For it is sufficient for the true unity of the Christian church that the gospel be preached in conformity with a pure understanding of it and that the sacraments be administered in accordance with the divine word. It is not necessary for the true unity of the Christian church that humanly instituted ceremonies should be observed uniformly in all places.

Augsburg Confession VII (1530)

The church earnestly desires that all the faithful be led to that full, conscious and active participation in liturgical celebrations called by the very nature of the liturgy. Such participation by the Christian people as "a chosen race, a royal priesthood, a holy nation, God's own people" (1 Pet. 2:9; see 2:4-5) is their right and duty by reason of their baptism.

Constitution on the Liturgy, Second Vatican Council (1963)

The services of the *Lutheran Book of Worship* embody the tradition of worship which received its characteristic shape during the early centuries of the church's existence and was reaffirmed during the Reformation era...

Freedom and flexibility in worship is a Lutheran inheritance, and there is room for ample variety in ceremony, music and liturgical form. Having considered their resources and their customs, congregations will find their own balance between fully using the ritual and musical possibilities of the liturgy, and a more modest practice. A full service should not allow secondary ceremonies to eclipse central elements of the liturgy, nor should a simple service omit essential or important parts.

Every service, whether elaborate or spare, sung or said, should be within the framework of the common rite of the church, so that the integrity of the rite is always respected and maintained.

The Structure
of the Eucharistic Service

1. Holy Communion: The Shape of the Rite

For Sunday is the primary day on which the church assembles: the first day of creation when God transformed darkness into light and the day on which Christ rose from death and revealed himself to the disciples in the scriptures and the breaking of the bread. The baptized gather to hear the word, to pray for those in need, to offer thanks to God for the gift of salvation, to receive the bread of life and the cup of blessing, and to be renewed for the daily witness of faith, hope and love. To guests, strangers, and all in need, the church offers these good things of God's grace.

Gathering

Entrance hymn
GREETING*
Kyrie
Hymn of praise
PRAYER OF THE DAY*

> (*In original in uppercase letters, with explanatory note as follows: "Central elements of the holy communion liturgy are noted in uppercase letters; other elements support and reveal the essential shape of Christian worship.")

God calls and gathers believers through the Holy Spirit, and in response the community acclaims this gracious God in song and prayer. The gathering of the congregation may begin with a confession of sin and/or an entrance hymn. God's welcome is extended to the congregation by the presider. When appropriate, a litany or hymn of praise may be sung immediately before the prayer of the day. Through these actions, the congregation prepares to hear the word of God.

Word

FIRST READING
Psalm
Second reading
Gospel acclamation
GOSPEL
SERMON

HYMN OF THE DAY
CREED
THE PRAYERS

In the rich treasure of scripture proclaimed by readers and preachers, the church hears the good news of God acting in this and every time and place. A three-year cycle of readings provides portions of the Hebrew scriptures, the New Testament letters, and the gospel books for each week. During Advent/Christmas, the lectionary reveals the mystery of the Word made flesh. In Lent/Easter, the paschal mystery of the Lord's death and resurrection is proclaimed. Throughout the season after Pentecost, the New Testament texts are read in a continuous order. During the last Sundays of the year, the readings present the final vision of a new heaven and a new earth.

This encounter with the living Word, Jesus Christ, is marked by proclamation and silence, psalm and hymn, singing and speaking, movement and gesture. Silence after the readings allows time for the word to be pondered. The sermon announces good news for the community and the world; the hymn of the day both proclaims and responds to the word; a creed is a further response to it. God's word, read and preached and acclaimed, leads the community to pray for the church, the people of the world, and those who suffer or are in need.

Meal

GREETING OF PEACE
PRESENTATION OF THE GIFTS
GREAT THANKSGIVING
LORD'S PRAYER
COMMUNION
Canticle
Prayer

In the thanksgiving, the congregation praises God for the gracious gifts of creation and the saving deeds of Jesus Christ. To the table of the Lord are brought bread and wine, simple signs of God's love, humble signs of human labour. In word and gesture, prayer and song, the people lift up their hearts in praise and thanksgiving for the gifts of forgiveness, life and salvation, hearing Jesus' words spoken at this supper, remembering his death and resurrection. The presider asks that the Holy Spirit unite the community in the Lord's bread and cup so that, as one body in Christ, it too might proclaim God's salvation in the world. To this grateful proclamation, the community joins its "Amen" before praying the Lord's prayer with one voice. Welcomed to the table, each one is united with God in Christ, with each other, and with the church's mission in the world. During the communion, hymns, songs and psalms may be sung. As the table is cleared, the congregation may sing a canticle. A brief prayer concludes the liturgy of the meal.

Sending

BLESSING
Dismissal

Worship on the Lord's day ends with simplicity. The community receives the blessing of God. All are invited to leave in peace, sent out to serve in word and deed: to speak the words of good news they have heard, to care for those in need, and to share what they have received with the poor and the hungry.

2. Basic Movement of the Service for the Lord's Day

With its focus upon scripture and sacrament, the main body of the service moves broadly from hearing to doing, from proclamation to thanksgiving, and from word to table.

Gathering: The people gather in response to God's call, offering praise in words of scripture, prayer and song. The people acknowledge their sinfulness and receive the declaration of God's forgiveness.

The word: Scriptures are read and their message is proclaimed. Psalms, hymns, spirituals or anthems may be sung between the readings. Responses to the proclamation of God's word include expressions of faith and commitment, and the offering of prayers for worldwide and local needs.

The eucharist: As hearing becomes doing, the tithes and offering of the people are gathered, *and the table is set with bread and wine. The people are invited to the table of the Lord.* Prayer is offered in which God is praised for creation and providence, Christ's work of redemption is remembered with thanksgiving, and the Holy Spirit invoked upon and in the church. *The bread is broken, and the bread and wine are served to the people.*

Sending: The people are sent forth with God's blessing to serve.

3. An Outline of the Service for the Lord's Day

Gathering

Call to worship
Prayer of the day or opening prayer
Hymn of praise, psalm or spiritual
Confession and pardon
The peace
Canticle, psalm, hymn or spiritual

The word

Prayer for illumination
First reading
Psalm
Second reading
Anthem, hymn, psalm, canticle or spiritual
Gospel reading
Sermon
Invitation
Affirmation of faith
(Pastoral rite of the church)
Prayers of the people
(The peace)

> *If the Lord's supper is not celebrated:*
> Offering
> Prayer of thanksgiving
> Lord's prayer

The eucharist

Offering
Invitation to the Lord's table
Great thanksgiving
Lord's prayer
Breaking of the bread
Communion of the people

Sending

Hymn, spiritual, canticle or psalm
Charge and blessing

4. An Order for Celebrating the Holy Eucharist

This rite requires careful preparation by the priest and other participants. It is not intended for use at the principal Sunday or weekly celebration of the holy eucharist.

The people and priest

Gather in the Lord's name

Proclaim and respond to the word of God
The proclamation and response may include readings, song, talk, dance, instrumental music, other art forms, silence. A reading from the gospels is always included.

Pray for the world and the church

Exchange the peace

Either here or elsewhere in the service, all greet one another in the name of the Lord.

Prepare the table

Some of those present prepare the table; the bread, the cup of wine, and other offerings, are placed upon it.

Make eucharist

The Great Thanksgiving is said by the priest in the name of the gathering, using one of the eucharistic prayers provided.

The people respond – Amen!

Break the bread

Share the gifts of God

The body and blood of the Lord are shared in a reverent manner; after all have received, any of the sacrament that remains is then consumed.

When a common meal or agape is part of the celebration, it follows here.

Eucharistic Prayers:
Ancient and Contemporary

1. Eucharistic Prayer from the Apostolic Tradition *of Hippolytus of Rome, ca. 215 CE*

The Lord be with you.
And also with you.

Lift up your hearts.
We lift them to the Lord.

Let us give thanks to the Lord our God.
It is right to give our thanks and praise.

We give you thanks, O God,
through your beloved Servant, Jesus Christ,
whom you have sent in these last times
as saviour and redeemer and messenger of your will.

He is your Word, inseparable from you,
through whom you made all things
and in whom you take delight.

He is your Word,
sent from heaven to a virgin's womb.
Being there conceived,
he took on our nature and our lot
and was shown forth as your Son,
born of the Holy Spirit and of the virgin Mary.

It is he who fulfilled all your will
and won for you a holy people:
he stretched out his hands in suffering
in order to free from suffering
those who put their trust in you.

It is he who,
handed over to a death he freely accepted,
in order to destroy death
and shatter the bonds of the evil one,
to crush hell underfoot
and lead the righteous into light,
to establish the boundary of hell

and manifest the resurrection,
taking bread and giving thanks to you, said:
"Take, eat, this is my body broken for you."

In the same way, also, the cup, saying:
"This is my blood poured out for you.
When you do this, do it for the remembrance of me."

Remembering therefore his death and resurrection,
we set before you this bread and cup,
giving you thanks that you have made us worthy
to stand before you and to serve you as priests.

And we ask you:
Send your Holy Spirit
upon the offering of the holy church.
Gather into one all who share these holy things,
Filling them with the Holy Spirit
to establish their faith in truth,
that together we may praise and glorify you
through your Servant, Jesus Christ.

Through him all glory and honour are yours, almighty Father,
with the Holy Spirit, in the holy church,
both now and forever.
Amen.

2. Eucharistic Prayer Adapted from the Alexandrine Liturgy of St Basil, 4th century CE

Since the words of institution are included in this prayer, they are not said in the invitation to the Lord's table, or in relation to the breaking of the bread.

The Lord be with you.
And also with you.

Lift up your hearts.
We lift them to the Lord.

Let us give thanks to the Lord our God.
It is right to give our thanks and praise.

It is truly right to glorify you, Father,
and to give you thanks,
for you alone are God, living and true,
dwelling in light inaccessible from before time and forever.

Fountain of all life and source of all goodness,

you made all things and fill them with your blessing;
you created them to rejoice in the splendour of your radiance.

Countless throngs of angels stand before you
to serve you night and day,
and, beholding the glory of your presence,
they offer you unceasing praise.
Joining with them,
and giving voice to every creature under heaven,
we glorify your name
and lift our voices in joyful praise:

The people may sing or say:

Holy, holy, holy Lord, God of power and might,
heaven and earth are full of your glory.
Hosanna in the highest.

Blessed is he who comes in the name of the Lord.
Hosanna in the highest.

We acclaim you, holy God, glorious in power;
your mighty works reveal your wisdom and love.
You formed us in your own image,
giving the whole world into our care,
so that, in obedience to you, our Creator,
we might rule and serve all your creatures.
When our disobedience took us far from you,
you did not abandon us to the power of death.
In your mercy you came to our help,
so that in seeking you we might find you.
Again and again you called us into covenant with you,
and through the prophets you taught us to hope for salvation.

Almighty God, you loved the world so much
that in the fullness of time you sent your only Son to be our Saviour.
Incarnate by the Holy Spirit, born of the Virgin Mary,
he lived as one of us, yet without sin.
To the poor he proclaimed the good news of salvation;
to prisoners, freedom;
to the sorrowful, joy.
To fulfil your purpose he gave himself up to death;
and, rising from the grave, destroyed death
and made the whole creation new.

And that we might live no longer for ourselves
but for him who died and rose for us,
God sent the Holy Spirit,
God's first gift for those who believe,
to complete God's work in the world,
and to bring to fulfilment the sanctification of all.

When the hour had come for him to be glorified
by you, his heavenly Father,
having loved his own who were in the world,
he loved them to the end:
at supper with them he took bread,
and after giving thanks to you,
he broke it, and gave it to his disciples, saying:
Take, eat.
This is my body, which is given for you.
Do this for the remembrance of me.

After supper he took the cup, saying:
This cup is the new covenant sealed in my blood,
shed for you and for all for the forgiveness of sins.
Whenever you drink it,
do it for the remembrance of me.

Holy God, we now celebrate this memorial of our redemption.
Recalling Christ's death and his descent among the dead,
proclaiming his resurrection and ascension to your right hand,
awaiting his coming in glory;
and offering to you, from the gifts you have given us,
this bread and this cup,
we praise you and we bless you.

The people may sing or say:

We praise you, we bless you,
we give thanks to you,
and we pray to you, Lord our God.

The minister continues:

Lord, we pray that in your goodness and mercy
your Holy Spirit may descend upon us, and upon these gifts,
sanctifying them and showing them to be holy gifts for your holy people,
the bread of life and the cup of salvation,
the body and blood of your Son Jesus Christ.

Grant that all who share this bread and this cup
may become one body and one spirit,
a living sacrifice in Christ,
to the praise of your name.

Remember, Lord, your one holy catholic and apostolic church,
redeemed by the blood of your Christ.
Reveal its unity, guard its faith,
and preserve it in peace.
    (Remember [N. and] all who minister in your church.)
    (Remember all your people, and those who seek your truth.)
    (Remember...)
    (Remember all who have died in the peace of Christ,

and those whose faith is known to you alone,
    bring them into the place of eternal joy and light.)

And grant that we may find our inheritance with
    (the blessed Virgin Mary, with patriarchs, prophets, apostles,
    and martyrs, and…)

all the saints who have found favour with you in ages past.
We praise you in union with them and give you glory through your Son,
Jesus Christ our Lord.

Through Christ, and with Christ, and in Christ,
all honour and glory are yours, almighty God and Father,
in the unity of the Holy Sprit,
forever and ever. Amen.

3. Great Thanksgiving

The Lord's table having been set, the one presiding then feeds the people in great thanksgiving. This prayer with its emphasis on thankful praise has been of central importance to this sacrament from very early centuries in Christian worship. Thanksgiving is so important to this sacrament that it has been given the name of *eucharist* (from the New Testament Greek word *eucharistia*, meaning thanksgiving).

We praise God for all God's mighty acts in the past, present and future.

God is praised for:
creating all things,
the providence of God,
establishing the covenant,
giving the law,
the witness of the prophets,
God's boundless love and mercy in spite of human failure,
the ultimate gift of Christ,
the immediate occasion or festival.

There may be an acclamation of praise, in which we join in one voice, with choirs of angels and with the faithful of every time and place, in adoration of the triune God: "Holy, holy, holy Lord", the song of the heavenly hosts, eternally being sung before God's majesty (Isa. 6:1-5).

Christ's work of redemption is recalled with thanks:
his birth, life and ministry,
his death and resurrection,
the promise of his coming again,
the gift of the sacrament (which may include the words of institution
if not otherwise used).

There may be an acclamation of faith, in which we joyfully acclaim Christ who died, is risen, and will come again.

The Holy Spirit is called upon
    to draw the people into the presence of the risen Christ,
    and to make the breaking of the bread and sharing of the cup
    a communion in the body and blood of Christ,
    that the people may be
    nourished with Christ's body,
    made one with the risen Christ,
    united with all the faithful in heaven and earth,
    kept faithful as Christ's body, representing Christ in ministry in the world,
    in anticipation of the fulfilment of the kingdom Christ proclaimed.

The prayer concludes with an ascription of praise to the triune God.

4. Great Thanksgiving

Since the words of institution are included in this prayer, they are not said in the invitation to the Lord's table, or in relation to the breaking of the bread.

The Lord be with you.
And also with you.

Lift up your hearts.
We lift them to the Lord.

Let us give thanks to the Lord our God.
It is right to give our thanks and praise.

Blessed are you, strong and faithful God.
All your works, the height and the depth,
echo the silent music of your praise.

In the beginning your Word summoned light,
night withdrew, and creation dawned.
As ages passed unseen,
waters gathered on the face of the earth
and life appeared.

When the times at last had ripened
and the earth grown full in abundance,
you created in your image man and woman,
the stewards of all creation.

You gave us breath and speech,
that all the living

might find a voice to sing your praise,
and to celebrate the creation you call good.
So now, with all the powers of heaven and earth,
we sing the ageless hymn of your glory:

The people may sing or say:

Holy, holy, holy Lord, God of power and might,
heaven and earth are full of your glory.
Hosanna in the highest.

Blessed is he who comes in the name of the Lord.
Hosanna in the highest.

The minister continues:

All holy God,
how wonderful is the work of your hands!
When sin had scarred the world,
you entered into covenant to renew the whole creation.

As a mother tenderly gathers her children,
as a father joyfully welcomes his own,
you embraced a people as your own
and filled them with longing
for a peace that would last
and for a justice that would never fail.

Through countless generations
your people hungered for the bread of freedom.
From them you raised up Jesus, your Son,
the living bread, in whom ancient hungers are satisfied.
He healed the sick,
though he himself would suffer;
he offered life to sinners,
though death would hunt him down.
But with a love stronger than death,
he opened wide his arms
and surrendered his spirit.

On the night before he met with death,
Jesus came to the table with those he loved.
He took bread
and praised you, God of all creation.
He broke the bread among his disciples and said:
Take this, all of you, and eat it.
This is my body, given for you.

When the supper was ended,
he took a cup of wine
and gave thanks to you, God of all creation.
He passed the cup among his disciples and said:

Take this, all of you, and drink from it.
This is the cup of the new covenant sealed in my blood
for the forgiveness of sin.
Do this in remembrance of me.

Gracious God, we offer you our sacrifice of praise and thanksgiving,
we commemorate Jesus, your Son.
Death could not bind him,
for you raised him up in the Spirit of holiness
and exalted him as Lord of creation.

The people may sing or say one of the following:

1. Great is the mystery of faith:

Christ has died,
Christ has risen,
Christ will come again.

2. Praise to you, Lord Jesus:

Dying you destroyed our death,
Rising you restored our life.
Lord Jesus, come in glory.

3. According to his commandment:

We remember his death,
We proclaim his resurrection,
We await his coming in glory.

4. Christ is the bread of life:

When we eat this bread and drink this cup,
we proclaim your death, Lord Jesus,
until you come in glory.

The minister continues:

Eternal God,
let your Holy Spirit move in power over us
and over these earthly gifts of bread and wine,
that they may be the communion of the body and blood of Christ,
and that we may become one in him.

May his coming in glory find us
ever watchful in prayer,
strong in truth and love,
and faithful in the breaking of the bread.

Then, at last, all peoples will be free,
all divisions healed,
and with your whole creation,
we will sing your praise,
through your Son, Jesus Christ.

Through Christ, with Christ, in Christ,
in the unity of the Holy Spirit,
all glory and honour are yours, Almighty Father,
forever and ever. Amen.

Lord's prayer

Following the great thanksgiving, the Lord's Prayer is said by the people.

5. Eucharistic Prayer

P. It is indeed right,
from east to west, from north to south,
in all the seasons of our life,
to give thanks to you, O God, O Living One.

(use this sentence or replace with proper preface:)
Dwelling beyond time and space, you abide among us,
embracing the world with your justice and love.

And so, with all the baptized of every race and land,
with the multitudes in heaven
and the countless choirs of angels,
we praise your glorious name
and join their unending hymn:

C. *Holy, holy, holy Lord God of power and might,*
Heaven and earth are full of your glory.
Hosanna in the highest.
Blessed is he who comes in the name of the Lord.
Hosanna in the highest.

P. Holy God,
holy and mighty one,
holy and immortal;
you we praise and glorify,
you we worship and adore.

You formed the earth from chaos;
you encircled the globe with air;
you created fire for warmth and light;
you nourish the lands with water.

You moulded us in your image,
and with mercy higher than the mountains,
with grace deeper than the sense,
you blessed the Israelites
and cherished them as your own.

That also we, estranged and dying,
might be adopted to live in your Spirit,
you called to us through the life and death of Jesus,
who in the night in which he was betrayed,
took bread, and gave thanks;
broke it, and gave it to his disciples,
saying: Take and eat; this is my body, given for you.
Do this for the remembrance of me.

Again, after supper,
he took the cup, gave thanks,
and gave it for all to drink,
saying: This cup is
the new covenant in my blood,
shed for you and for all people
for the forgiveness of sin.
Do this for the remembrance of me.

Together as the body of Christ,
we proclaim the mystery of his death:

C. *Christ has died. Christ is risen. Christ will come again.*

P. With this bread and cup we remember your Son,
the first-born of your new creation.
We remember his life lived for others,
and his death and resurrection,
which renew the face of the earth.
We await his coming
when, with the world made perfect through your wisdom,
all our sins and sorrow will be no more.

C. *Amen. Come, Lord Jesus.*

P. Holy God,
holy and merciful one,
holy and compassionate,
send upon us and this meal
your Holy Spirit,
whose breath revives us for life,
whose fire rouses us to love.
Enfold in your arms all who share this holy food.
Nurture in us the fruits of the Spirit,
that we may be a living tree,
sharing your bounty with all the world.

C. *Amen. Come, Holy Spirit.*

P. Holy and benevolent God,
receive our praise and petitions,
as Jesus received the cry of the needy,
and fill us with your blessing,
until, needy no longer and bound to you in love,

we feast forever in the triumph of the Lamb;
through whom all glory and honour is yours.
O God, O Living One,
with the Holy Spirit,
in your holy church, now and forever.
C. Amen.

6. Eucharistic Prayer

Celebrant   The grace of our Lord Jesus Christ and the love of God and the fellowship of the Holy Spirit be with you all.
People   *And also with you.*
Celebrant   Lift up your hearts.
People   *We lift them to the Lord.*
Celebrant   Let us give thanks to the Lord our God.
People   *It is right to give him thanks and praise.*

The celebrant
gives thanks to God the Father for his work in creation and his revelation of himself to his people;
recalls before God, when appropriate, the particular occasion being celebrated;
incorporates or adapts the proper preface of the day, if desired.
If the sanctus is to be included, it is introduced with these or similar words:
And so we join the saints and angels in proclaiming your glory, and we sing(say):

Celebrant and people
Holy, holy, holy Lord, God of power and might,
heaven and earth are full of your glory.
Hosanna in the highest.
Blessed is he who comes in the name of the Lord.
Hosanna in the highest.

The celebrant now praises God for the salvation of the world through Jesus Christ our Lord.

At the following words concerning the bread, the celebrant is to hold it, or lay a hand upon it; and at the words concerning the cup, to hold or place a hand upon the cup and any other vessel containing wine to be consecrated.

On the night he was handed over to suffering and death, our Lord Jesus Christ took bread; and when he had given thanks to you, be broke it, and gave it to his disciples, and said, "Take, eat: This is my body, which is given for you. Do this for the remembrance of me."

After supper he took the cup of wine; and when he had given thanks, he gave it to them, and said, "Drink this, all of you: This is my blood of the new covenant, which is shed for you and for many for the forgiveness of sins. Whenever you drink it, do this for the remembrance of me."

Recalling now his suffering and death, and celebrating his resurrection and ascension, we await his coming in glory.

Accept, O Lord, our sacrifice of praise, this memorial of our redemption.

Send your Holy Spirit upon these gifts. Let them be for us the body and blood of your Son. And grant that we who eat this bread and drink this cup may be filled with your life and goodness.

The celebrant then prays that all may receive the benefits of Christ's work, and the renewal of the Holy Spirit.

The prayer concludes with these or similar words:

All this we ask through your Son Jesus Christ. By him, and with him, and in him, in the unity of the Holy Spirit all honour and glory is yours, Almighty Father, now and for ever. Amen.

The Invocation of the Spirit

JOHN H. MCKENNA

Conclusions

Having looked at the data, I now invite you to reflect on the implications. The starting point is the epiclesis in the early Christian texts. While in no way providing an inflexible norm, these texts do provide us with a basis for comparison.

Some general characteristics seem evident. One is the reference to some change in the bread and wine in the direction of Christ's body and blood. Another is the frequent appearance of the eschatological dimension and the rich variety of "other benefits". Finally, there is almost invariably a reference to partaking of the gifts.

The epicleses in the *Book of Common Prayer* seem to exhibit no significant variances from this pattern. One might simply note that had the term "word" been left as Cranmer intended it, as a reference to the institution narrative rather than the incarnate Word, we might have a compromise form which would draw us closer to the earthly Christian emphases. This viewed the eucharistic prayer in its entirety as "consecratory", with two highpoints – the institution narrative and the epiclesis.[59]

The Lutheran epicleses reveal a significant variation. There is no reference to a change of the bread and wine into the body and blood of Christ. This element is characteristic of most early epicleses. It is absence due to an emphasis on the institution narrative as "consecratory" or a desire to avoid the implications of certain terms – or both? On the other hand, the Lutheran prayers show a strong sense of the eschatological dimension.

The Methodist epicleses reveal an emphasis on calling down the Spirit upon the people. The eschatological note is missing in the first six great thanksgivings but is present in the next sixteen – mainly because they use number seven as a prototype. The text made official in May 1984 has a strong eschatological emphasis and is probably the most complete resumé of elements traditionally associated with the epiclesis. It also forcefully underlines the transformation of the gifts as well as the assembly.

The Presbyterian prayers also show a great awareness of the calling down of the Spirit upon the people as well as the gifts. The eschatological dimension is lacking in most of the epicleses. The option to say the institution narrative with the breaking of the bread – thus placing the epiclesis before the institution narrative – is a significant variant from the ancient pattern.

The Roman Catholic pattern is perhaps the most problematic when compared to the early Christian epicleses. Here we find the stress on the unity of those partaking which is common to many of the modern epicleses and a good number of the ancient ones. The "split" epiclesis, however, is found only in the Alexandrian type of earlier prayers and is an isolated phenomenon among more modern ones. Most probably this is a vestige of the old (but *not* ancient) "moment of consecration" problem and the fear that mentioning a change in the gifts *after* the institution narrative would somehow rob the latter of its consecratory power.

Unfortunately, this pattern has several disadvantages. It neglects the stronger of the ancient traditions. It also interrupts the flow of the narration of the wonderful things God has accomplished in creation and in history. It fails to emphasize the basic helplessness or praying attitude of the assembly and thus fails to help avoid a "magical" notion of the institution narrative. Finally, this pattern could rob the epiclesis of one of its greatest strengths, viz., the ability to underline the unity between "consecration" and communion.[60] The fact that this pattern continues to be imposed on Roman Catholic eucharistic prayers[61] calls for serious reconsideration.

The changing of the gifts into Christ's body and blood finds forceful emphasis in the Roman Catholic epicleses. There is, however, no trace of an eschatological dimension (which appears in the intercessions following the epiclesis) and, besides unity, other benefits to those partaking are extremely sparse.

Obviously, the epiclesis is only one element in the eucharistic prayers and to isolate it, as we have done in this study, is to risk onesidedness. Nevertheless, a comparison of the epiclesis in different traditions is revealing. At times, it shows contrasting mentalities, if not theological biases. At other times, it reveals the fruit of ecumenical dialogue and scholarship. One can only hope that this latter will yield further enrichment for all traditions and lead us closer to that day when Christ's final victory and the unity for which the epiclesis so often prays will become a reality.

NOTES

[59] Cf. McKenna, *Eucharist and Holy Spirit* (= Alcuin Club Collections #57), Great Wakering, Mayew-McCrimmon, 1975, pp. 48-71, esp. 69-71.

[60] *Ibid.*, pp. 206-207.

[61] Cf. *An Original Eucharistic Prayer: Text 1*, Washington, DC, International Committee on English in the Liturgy, 1984, p.11 and pp.13-14. An earlier version read: "May the Spirit of holiness move among us always inspiring our vision and guiding our hearts in union with N., our pope, N., our bishop, and all who preach the gospel of peace to the poor." This second petition, perhaps in an effort towards brevity, seems to have been swallowed up in the prayers which preceded and followed it.

V

Appendices

Participants

Ms Clara **Ajo Lazaro**, Rua Russia 621/17, Taboao, S.B. do Campo, SP, 09872-000, Brazil

Rev. Mary **Au**, Calvary Church, 6 Shatin Pass Road, Kowloon, Hong Kong

Rev. Dr Janet **Crawford**, College of St John the Evangelist, Private Bag 28-907, Remuera, Auckland 1136, Aotearoa New Zealand

Ms Marja **de Groot**, Nogenoord 13, 3513 6X Utrecht, The Netherlands

Mr Juan A. **Gattinoni**, Tres Arroyos 1896, Case postale, 1416 Buenos Aires, Argentina

Rev. Dr Robert W. **Gribben**, 22 Illawarra Road, North Balwyn, Victoria 3104, Australia

Rev. Per **Harling**, Box 92, 193 22 Sigtuna, Sweden

Rev. Dr Dennis **Hughes**, PCUSA, 100 Witherspoon Street, Rm 2616, Louisville, Kentucky 40202, USA

Ms G. Denise **Isaac**, P. O. Box 48, Victoria Road, Bassetterre, St Kitts, West India

Fr Brian **Jemmott**, Curate's Flat, Holy Trinity Cathedral, 30A Abercromby Street, Port of Spain, Trinidad

Rev. Gerd **Kerl**, Flughafenstr. 69b, 44309 Dortmund, Germany

Ms Aileen **Khoo**, 6 Jalan 5/37, 46000 Petaling Jaya, Selangor, Malaysia

Rev. Stephen **Larson**, 2 chemin de la Bride, 1224 Chêne-Bougeries, Switzerland

Rev. Prof. Gordon **Lathrop**, Lutheran Theological Seminary, 7301 Germantown Avenue, Philadelphia, PA 19119, USA

Dr Janice **Long**, 9845 Cunningham Road, Cincinatti, OH 45243, USA

Rev. Paul **Long**, 6000 Drake Road, Cincinatti, OH 45243, USA

Rev. Dr Jaci **Maraschin**, Rua Leão XIII, no 230 ap 11, Rudge Ramos, SB do Campo, 09735-220 São Paulo, Brazil

Rev. Romeu **Martini**, IEPG, CP 14, 93001-970 São Leopoldo, RS, Brazil

Mr Patrick **Matsikenyiri**, Africa University, P.O. Box 1320, Mutara, Zimbabwe

Rev. Rodney **Matthews**, ACTS, Scottish Churches House, Dunblane, FK15 OAJ, Scotland

Ms Joan **Matthews** (c/o ACTS, as above)

Rev. Bettina **Naumann**, Schiersandstr. 34, 09116 Chemnitz, Germany

Fr José **Nixon**, Philippine Independent Church, 1500 Taft Avenue, Ermita, Manila, Philippines 1000

Mr Kurt **Rose**, Albert-Schweitzer-Str. 72, 29223 Celle, Germany

Rev. J. **Saragih**, ITAS Medan, Jl Binjai Km 10, 8 Desa Paya, Geli Medan Sunggal 20352, Indonesia

Ms Maria **Simeone**, Rua Antonio Emanuelli, 48 apto 303, Garibaldi RS, Brazil

Rev. Dr Anita **Stauffer**, Lutheran World Federation, 150 route de Ferney, P.O. Box 2100, 1211 Geneva 2, Switzerland.

Mr Wolfgang **Teichmann**, Mozartsstr. 3, 37586 Dassel, Germany

Fr Pathrose Elias **Thandikayil**, Ainat, Mulanthuruthy, Ernakulam 682 314, Kerala, India

Ms Eileen **Thompson**, Church of Bangladesh, 54 Johnson Road, Dhaka, Bangladesh

Rev. Pedro **Triana Fernandez**, Rua Russia 621/17, Taboao, S.B. do Campo, SP Brazil, CEP 09872-000

Rev. Atze **Veldhuis**, Harrow United Church, 955 Mulvey Avenue, Winnipeg, Manitoba R3M 1G8, Canada.

Ms Karen **Webster**, 19 Gresley Court, Acomb, York YO2 5PF, UK

Rev. Laura **van Weijen**, Bergweg 64, 6881 LT, Velpt, Netherlands

Staff

Rev. Dr Thomas F. **Best**, Faith and Order

Ms Roswitha **Ginglas-Poulet,** Bossey

Ms Renate **Guillemon,** Bossey

Rev. Dr Dagmar **Heller**, Faith and Order

Rev. Terry **MacArthur,** Worship and Spirituality

Rev. Dr Beate **Stierle,** Bossey

Ms Evelyne **Tatu,** Bossey

Sources

We wish to thank all those who have granted permission for the use of the following materials in this book. We have made every effort to identify their sources correctly, and to secure the necessary permissions for their use. We apologize for any unintended errors in the permissions statements or acknowledgments, or any unwitting infringement of copyright.

The acknowledgments for music are given following each piece. The bibliographical information for each source is followed by the permissions or acknowledgment statement for the text(s) used in this volume. The location of each text in this volume is indicated in bold type, followed by the title of the text and then, when appropriate, the location in the printed source.

1. *The Book of Common Prayer and Administration of the Sacraments and Other Rites and Ceremonies of the Church together with The Psalter or Psalms of David, According to the Use of the Episcopal Church* [place not given], Seabury Press, 1979.

> The materials are in the public domain; the above source is acknowledged.
>
> • pp. **145**: "An Order for Celebrating the Holy Eucharist"; pp.400-401.
>
> • pp. **157**: "Eucharistic Prayer" [At the Great Thanksgiving, Form 2]; pp.404-405.

2. *The Book of Common Worship*, prepared by the Theology and Worship Ministry Unit for the Presbyterian Church (USA) and the Cumberland Presbyterian Church, Louisville, Kentucky, Westminster/John Knox Press, 1993.

> From *The Book of Common Worship*. © 1993 Westminster/John Knox Press. Used by permission of Westminster John Knox Press.
>
> • pp. **144**: "Basic Movement of the Service for the Lord's Day"; p.33.
>
> • pp. **144**: "An Outline of the Service for the Lord's Day"; p.46.
>
> • pp. **151**: "Great Thanksgiving"; pp.42-43.

3. The Committee on a Common Eucharistic Liturgy

> Copyright © 1975 by Marion J. Hatchett, Chairman, Committee on a Common Eucharistic Liturgy. Used by permission.
>
> • pp. **148**: "Eucharistic Prayer Adapted from the Alexandrian Liturgy of St Basil, 4th century CE".

4. International Commission on English in the Liturgy

> Eucharistic Prayer A, copyright © 1986, International Committee on English in the Liturgy, Inc. Adapted and used with permission.
>
> • pp. **152**: "Great Thanksgiving".
>
> • pp. **147**: "Eucharistic Prayer from the *Apostolic Tradition* of Hippolytus of Rome, ca. 215 CE". (This version of the earliest extant full eucharistic prayer has been adapted from that appearing in the *Book of Common Worship* [Louisville, Westminster/John Knox, 1993], pp.150-51. Original translation and revisions by Gordon Lathrop.)

5. [Excerpted from] "The Epiclesis Revisited" by John H. McKenna, CM, in *New Eucharistic Prayers: An Ecumenical Study of Their Development and Structure*, Frank C. Senn, ed., New York, Paulist, 1987.

> From *New Eucharistic Prayers*, edited by Frank C. Senn 1987 by Frank C. Senn. Used by permission of Paulist Press.
>
> • pp. **159**: "The Invocation of the Spirit"; pp.182-83.

6. New Revised Standard Version of the Bible.

> Scriptural quotations are taken from the New Revised Standard Version (NRSV) Bible, 1989 by the Division of Christian Education of the National Council of the Churches of Christ in the United States of America.
>
> • pp. **140**: Luke 24:27, 30-31a and Acts 2:42.

7. Gail Ramshaw

> © by Gail Ramshaw. Used by permission.
>
> • pp. **155**: "Eucharistic Prayer".

8. *With One Voice: A Lutheran Resource for Worship*, Minneapolis, Augsburg Fortress, 1995.

> Reprinted by permission from *With One Voice*, copyright © 1995 Augsburg Fortress.
>
> • pp. **140**: "Foundations for the Christian Assembly"; pp.6-7.
>
> • pp. **142**: "Holy Communion: Shape of the Rite"; pp. 8-9.